Centerville Library
Washington-Centerville Public Library
Centerville, Ohio

DISCARD

#1
GRANNY OWL
Instructions: P.79

Introduction

Origami, or paper folding, has long been recognized as a hobby for children. It is fun to create a familiar figure simply by folding a square of origami paper, and when a project is done, you might want to keep it as a decoration. However, authentic origami figures are so light-weight and fragile they don't last long nor stand by themselves, and they were meant to be thrown away after all.

This book introduces you to an innovative approach to origami craft. The projects are heavy-weight and stable so you can keep them as ornaments. A small rectangular piece of paper is folded into a tiny, "magic" triangle. Make as many pieces as you can and build the figures or structures you fancy. You can suit your own sense by changing colors and numbers of pieces in certain rows, and by using paper of different thicknesses or textures. The possibilities are endless.

Origami is quite a time-consuming craft, but you need no special tools or workplace. With just paper and scissors, 3D origami is fun for all ages. In Japan, it has also become popular among people recovering after all illnesses. Everybody can enjoy folding and interlocking the "magic" triangles just as you would patchwork, knit or build with Lego® blocks.

DISTRIBUTORS

United States: Kodansha America, Inc. through Oxford University Press, 198 Madison Avenue, New York, NY 10016
Canada: Fitzhenry & Whiteside Ltd., 195 Allstate Parkway, Markham, Ontario L3R 4T8
United Kingdom and Europe: Premier Book Marketing Ltd., Clarendon House, 52, Cornmarket Street, Oxford, OX1 3HJ England
Australia and New Zealand: Bookwise International, 54 Crittenden Road, Findon, South Australia 5023 Australia
The Far East and Japan: Japan Publications Trading Co.,Ltd., 1-2-1, Sarugaku-cho, Chiyoda-ku, Tokyo 101-0064 Japan

First Edition July 2000, 2nd printing July 2001
Original Copyright©1999 Boutique-sha
World rights reserved by JOIE, INC., 1-8-3, Hirakawa-cho, Chiyoda-ku, Tokyo 102-0093 Japan

No part of this book or portions thereof may be reproduced in any form or by any means including electronic retrieval systems without prior written approval from the author or publisher.

Printed in Japan

ISBN4-88996-057-0

736.982
Thre

W9-DFS-256

3

ENJOY RECYCLING PAPERS

Our daily life is filled with various kinds of paper that are destined to be thrown away; catalogs, wrapping paper, magazines, tickets, flyers, etc. Before just getting rid of them, why don't you consider recycling them by creating delightful 3D figures? Save glossy, thick papers, patterned or solid, for later use.

GOOD-LUCK *HYOTAN*(GOURD): P.23

RED-CROWNED CRANE: P.21

PEDESTAL: P.21

HAT: P.15

TOOTHPICK HOLDER: P.15

FISH: P.10

TORTOISE: P.8

4

Since each basic rectangle should be less than 2" × 4", you can cut any size of used paper down to that size. Surprisingly beautiful effects will be obtained when patterned pieces are assembled together. This handicraft will be satisfying to you in a number of ways, learning a new skill, a constructive use of your time, and recycling unwanted paper into an artful new form.

BASKET: P.14

KINGFISHER: P.11

USING A VARIETY OF PAPERS

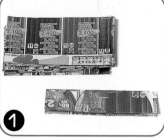

❶ Fold in half.

❷ Fold in half again.

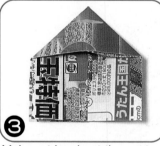

❸ Make a triangle at the center. (See P.28 for details).

❹ Fold in bottom corners.

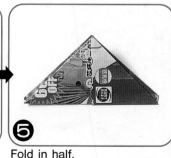

❺ Fold in half.

❽ Stack by inserting the points of triangles.

❼ Prepare necessary number of triangles.

❻ Fold in half again.

TO BEGIN

Any 3D origami project begins with a small triangular piece. First, let's see how the basic triangle is folded.

This is an easy example to give you the idea of how the basic piece is formed. See P.27-29 for more detailed instructions.

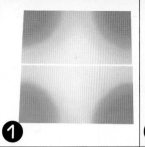

❶ Use one half of a square origami paper.

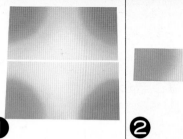

❷ Fold in half to make a thinner rectangle.

❸ Fold in half in the other direction.

❹ Fold up (upper flap) so the bottom edge aligns with the left.

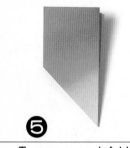

❺ Turn over and fold in the same manner.

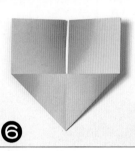

❻ Open as shown.

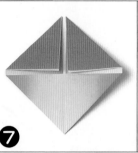

❼ Fold down upper corners.

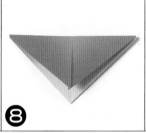

❽ Fold down in half.

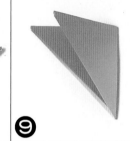

❾ Fold in half to complete a basic triangular piece.

There are 3 types of triangle, according to the project. See P.27-29 for more details.

Each of the three sides of the triangle has a different form of edge, which enables the crafter to vary the direction of inserting more pieces, creating 2D or 3D designs.

ORNAMENT STAND
Instructions for #2 & #3: P.32

#2

#3

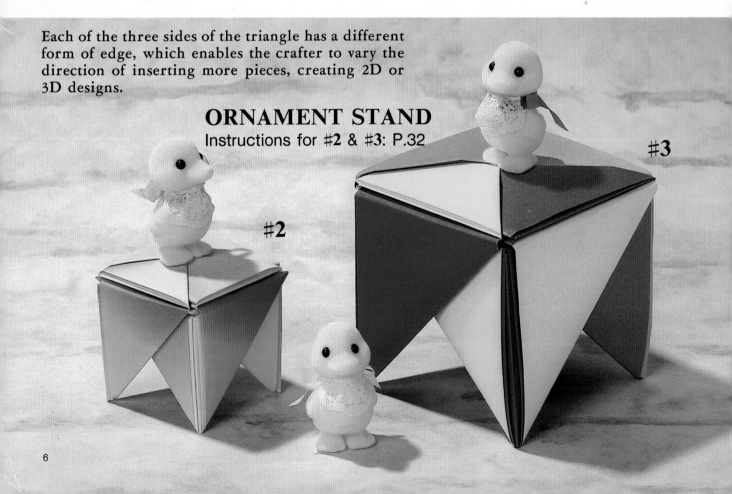

TWO-TONE RING

#5
TWO-TONE RING AND FROG
Instructions: P.30

#6
TWO-TONE RING AND GOLDFISH
Instructions: P.31

CHRISTMAS TREE

#4
TWO-TONE RING AND CRANE
Instructions: P.30

#7
FIR TREE
Instructions: P33

#8
TREE WITH LIGHTS
Instructions: P33

---

❶ RING ASSEMBLY

Hold the first piece with your left hand, the pockets facing you.

❷

Hold the second piece with your right hand so two pointed points face left.

❸

Insert two points into double pocket of the first piece.

❹

Insert deeply as shown.

❺

Insert two points of the third piece into double pocket.

❻

Continue so the pocket side alternates its angle, vertically and diagonally.

❼

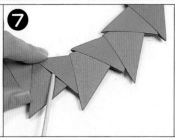

Apply a dash of glue between pieces, adjusting the shape.

❽

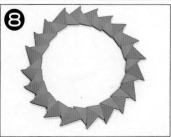

Completed RING.

Pieces used in the actual project are smaller. 7

Make as many as 40 triangles to create a beautiful tortoise. All you have to do is insert in the same direction. It's easy yet creative.

#9

#10

The above is made of wrapping paper.

TORTOISE

Instructions for #9–#15: P.5

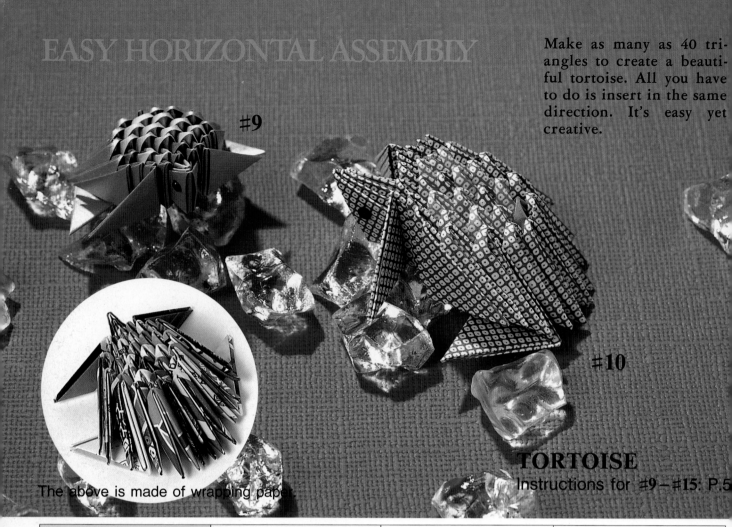

TORTOISE ASSEMBLY **Different colors are used here for easy comprehension.**	❶ Make 40 triangular pcs.	❷ Place 3 pcs. as Row 1, double pockets down. Join them with 4 pcs. by inserting double points into adjoining pockets of 2 pcs.	❸ Row 3: Insert 5 pcs.
❹ Row 4: Insert 6 pcs.	❺ Row 5: Insert 5 pcs., leaving side triangles unworked .	❻ Row 6: Insert 4 pcs.	❼ Row 7: Insert 3 pcs.

#12

#14

#11

#13

#15

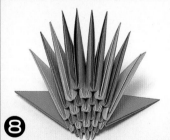 ⑧ Row 8: Insert 2 pcs.

 ⑨ Row 9: Put 1 pc. between 2 pcs. of Row 8, and glue to secure.

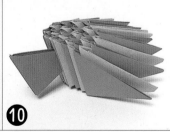 ⑩ Head: Insert 1 pc. into center piece of Row 1.

 ⑪ Cover with 1 pc. inserting into adjoining pockets.

 ⑫ Cover it again with 1 pc. inserting into outer pockets.

 ⑬ Fore legs: Open 1 pc. and insert one point into an outer pocket of Row 2. Repeat on the other side.

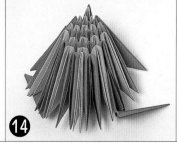 ⑭ Hind legs: Open 1 pc. and insert one point into an outer pocket of Row 6. Glue to secure. Repeat on the other side.

 ⑮ Glue on eyes to finish.

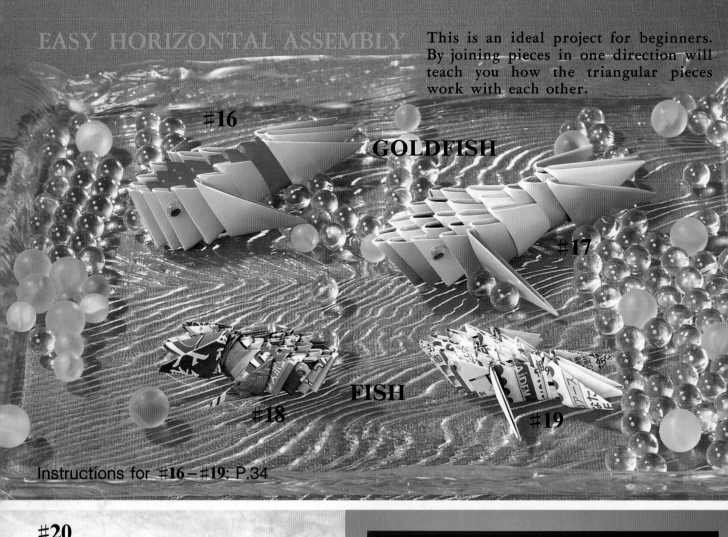

This is an ideal project for beginners. By joining pieces in one direction will teach you how the triangular pieces work with each other.

#16

GOLDFISH

#17

FISH

#18

#19

Instructions for #16 – #19: P.34

#20
SOARING CRANE
Instructions: P.36

10

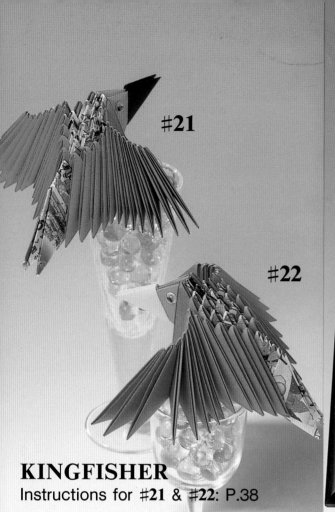

#21

#22

KINGFISHER
Instructions for **#21** & **#22**: P.38

#23
SWALLOW
Instructions: P.39

EASY HORIZONTAL ASSEMBLY

Most larger projects are constructed on a round base. Once you have learned the trick of the triangular pieces, this sunflower can be a good basis from which to start to proceed to more complicated designs. The more pieces you start with, the more easily you can join them, although the center hole will be enlarged as well. It is useful to practice joining small numbers of pieces securely.

#24

#25

SUNFLOWER
Instructions for #24 & #25: P.13

Completed size
6" diameter

Materials

#24: 54 2"x 3½" rectangles of craft paper (yellow)
     48 2"x 3½" rectangles of craft paper (browm)
#25: 54 2"x 3½" rectangles of craft paper (yellow)
     24 2"x 3½" rectangles of craft paper (black)
     24 2"x 3½" rectangles of craft paper (ocher)

Note
The completed project may look different depending on the thickness of the paper used.

①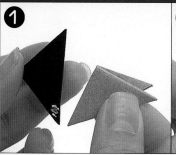

Apply a dab of glue onto the tip of the single point of a triangular piece.

②

Press 2 pcs. to secure.

③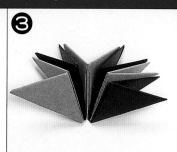

Repeat to make a 5-6 pc. cluster.

④

Make several clusters until 24 pcs. are joined. Join into a ring and glue to secure.

⑤

Interlock 1 pc. so as to covering the adjoining points.

⑥

3 pcs. are joined to the far side.

⑦

24 pcs. are joined all around.

⑧

Holding the double pocket side of a yellow piece, insert its points into adjoining pockets.

⑨

24 pcs. are inserted all around.

⑩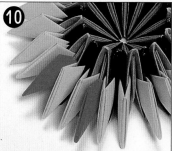

Increase petals by inserting 1 pc. into the opening between every 2 pcs.

⑪

Keep adding until 12 pcs. are inserted.

⑫

Now, the real color petals, 36 in all.

⑬

Hold the flower downside up, and insert a piece held at the double pocket into adjacent openings.

⑭

When 18 pcs. are added, turn over and adjust the angles of petals.

⑮

Secure by gluing the final row pieces from the back side.

⑯

Apply glue all over the back side and attach onto a cardboard.

13

THREE-DIMENSIONAL ASSEMBLY

First make a circular base with triangular pieces. Then stack upward to create a 3D project. Once you have mastered the construction of the first piece, which is a little tricky, various shapes can be constructed as you wish. Start with a small number of pieces and proceed to more elaborate designs using a larger number of pieces.

#27

#26

BASKET
Instructions for #26 & #27: P.40

TOOTHPICK HOLDER
Instructions for #28 – #30: P.35

#29

#30

#28

HAT
Instructions for #31 – #33: P.41

#32

#31

#33

Fold and save triangular pieces in your spare time, in assorted colors or patterns, and challenge yourself to grander projects shown here and on the following pages.

PINEAPPLE
Instructions for #34 & #35: P.42

#35

#34

#36

#37

MINI PINEAPPLE
Instructions for #36 & #37: P.44

Pedestal for Pineapple

FRUIT COMBO

**#38
WATERMELON**
Instructions: P.46

**#39
LEMON**
Instructions: P.67

**#40
STRAWBERRY**
Instructions: P.47

17

#41

#42

#43

ELEGANT CRANE
Instructions for #41 – #43: P.48

#45

#44

BABY SWAN
Instructions for #44 & #45: P.54

#46

#47

#48

SWAN
Instructions for #46 – #48: P.56

19

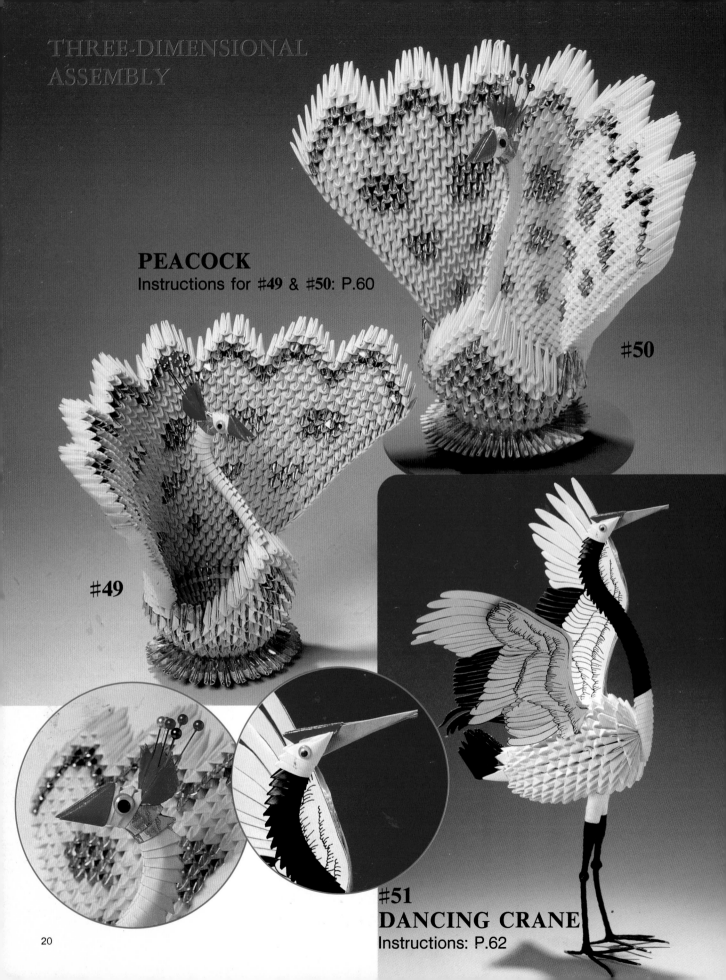

PEACOCK
Instructions for #49 & #50: P.60

#50

#49

#51
DANCING CRANE
Instructions: P.62

RED-CROWNED CRANE
Instructions for #52 & #53: P.52

#52

#53

#54
PEDESTAL
Instructions: P.53

21

METALLIC URN
Instructions for #55 & #56: P.88

#55

#56

TEMARI BALL
Instructions for #57 & #58: P.68

#58

#57

GOOD-LUCK *HYOTAN* (GOURD)
Instructions for #59 – #61: P.70

#59

#60

#61

OWL
Instructions for #62–#64: P.76

#62

#63

#64

#65

#66

#67

WINGED OWL
Instructions for #65–#67: P.72

24

#68
KAPPA
Instructions: P.80

PENGUIN
Instructions for #69 & #70: P.82

#70

#69

#71

#72

#73

#74

KITTEN
Instructions for #71 & #72: P.84

RABBIT
Instructions for #73 & #74: P.86

25

#75
BRIDEGROOM
Instructions: P.74

#76
BRIDE
Instructions: P.75

THREE-DIMENSIONAL ASSEMBLY

OWL WEDDING

#78

#77
RING BEARER
Instructions: P.78

#79
FLOWER GIRL
Instructions: P.78

HOW TO MAKE TRIANGULAR PIECES

● Using origami paper: Type "A"

The rectangular piece for Type "A" has an exact ratio of 2 : 1 for length to width because it is a half of square origami paper. Some projects require other types which have a slightly different ratio. (See P.28-29.)

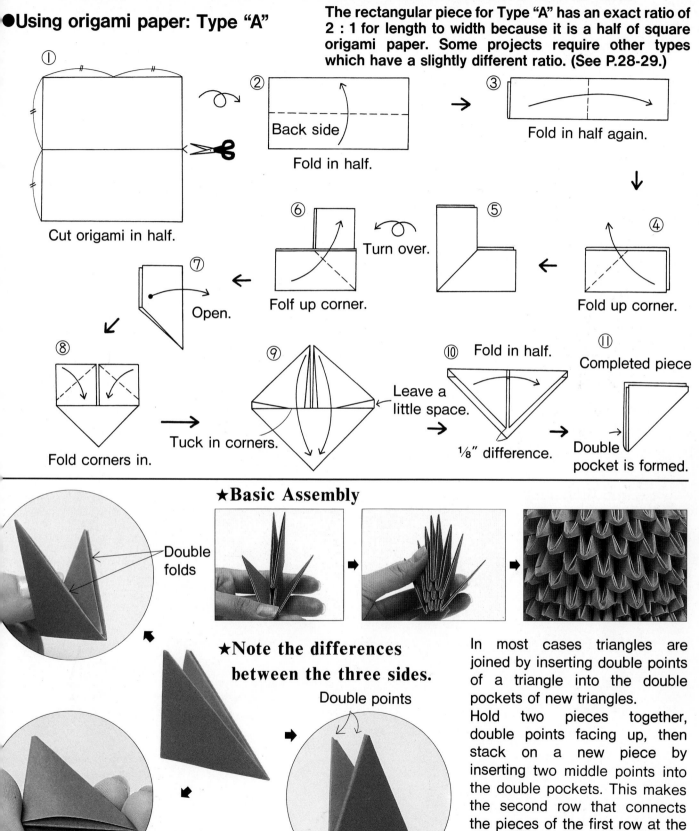

① Cut origami in half.

② Back side
Fold in half.

③ Fold in half again.

④ Fold up corner.

⑤

⑥ Folf up corner.

Turn over.

⑦ Open.

⑧ Fold corners in.

Tuck in corners.

⑨ Leave a little space.

⑩ Fold in half.
⅛" difference.

⑪ Completed piece
Double pocket is formed.

★Basic Assembly

Double folds

Double pocket

★Note the differences between the three sides.

Double points

In most cases triangles are joined by inserting double points of a triangle into the double pockets of new triangles.

Hold two pieces together, double points facing up, then stack on a new piece by inserting two middle points into the double pockets. This makes the second row that connects the pieces of the first row at the same time.

●**Using flyer or wrapping paper: Type "B"**

Usually commercial paper does not have the exact ratio of 2 to 1 for its length to width. So the width of Type "B" rectangle is slightly longer than a half of the length. This type piece is often useful.

[Cut into rectangles]

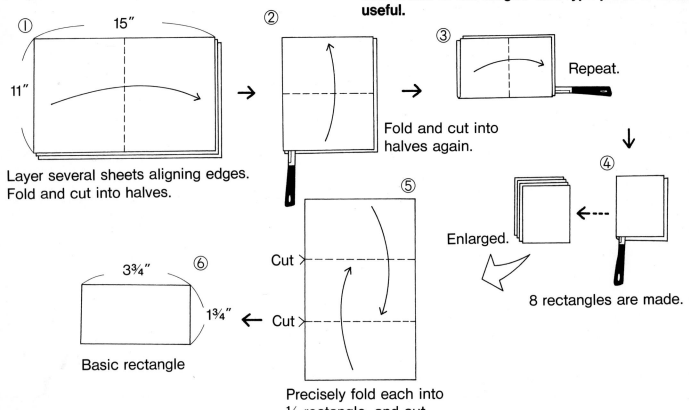

① 15″ 11″

Layer several sheets aligning edges. Fold and cut into halves.

②

③ Repeat.

Fold and cut into halves again.

④ Enlarged.

8 rectangles are made.

⑤ Cut → ← Cut

Precisely fold each into ⅓ rectangle, and cut.

⑥ 3¾″ 1¾″

Basic rectangle

[Fold into triangles]

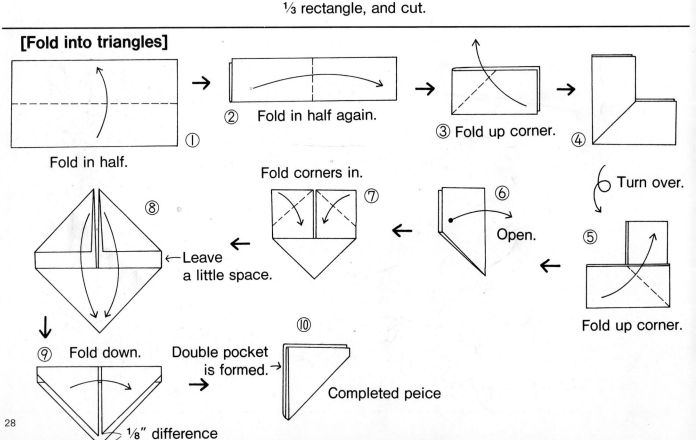

① Fold in half.

② Fold in half again.

③ Fold up corner.

④

Turn over.

⑤ Fold up corner.

⑥ Open.

⑦ Fold corners in.

⑧ ←Leave a little space.

⑨ Fold down.

⑩ Double pocket is formed.→

Completed peice

⅛″ difference

HOW TO MAKE TRIANGULAR PIECES

●**Using craft paper: Type "C"**

Commercial rectangular papers are available at handicraft shops. This Type "C" rectangle has a width slightly less than a half of the length.

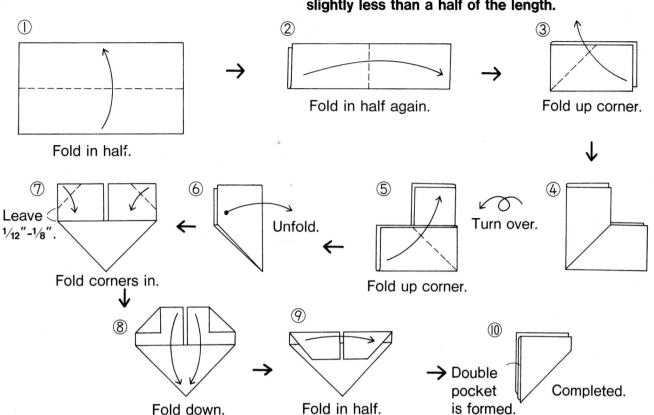

① Fold in half.

→

② Fold in half again.

→

③ Fold up corner.

↓

④

↶ Turn over.

⑤ Fold up corner.

←

⑥ Unfold.

←

⑦ Leave ¹⁄₁₂"-¹⁄₈". Fold corners in.

↓

⑧ Fold down.

→

⑨ Fold in half.

→ Double pocket is formed.

⑩ Completed.

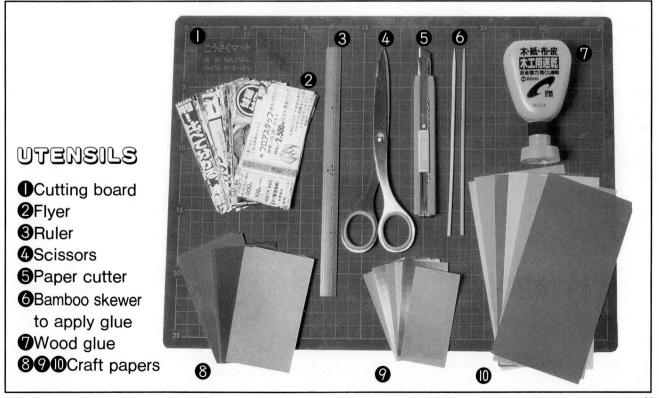

UTENSILS

❶Cutting board
❷Flyer
❸Ruler
❹Scissors
❺Paper cutter
❻Bamboo skewer to apply glue
❼Wood glue
❽❾❿Craft papers

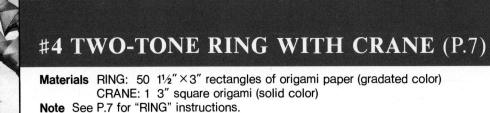

Materials RING: 50 1½"×3" rectangles of origami paper (gradated color)
CRANE: 1 3" square origami (solid color)
Note See P.7 for "RING" instructions.

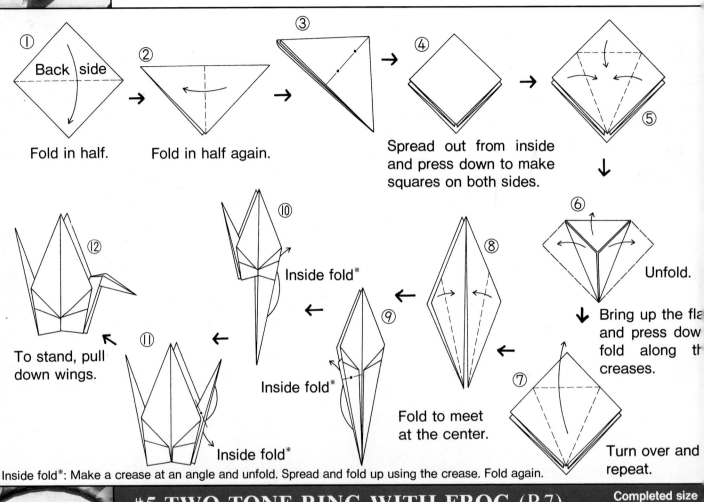

① Back side
Fold in half.

② Fold in half again.

③ →

④ Spread out from inside and press down to make squares on both sides.

⑤ ↓

⑥ Unfold.

↓ Bring up the fla
and press dow
fold along th
creases.

⑦ Turn over and repeat.

⑧ Fold to meet at the center.

⑨ Inside fold*

⑩ Inside fold*

⑪ Inside fold*

⑫ To stand, pull down wings.

Inside fold*: Make a crease at an angle and unfold. Spread and fold up using the crease. Fold again.

Materials RING: 52 1½"×3" rectangles of origami paper (gradated color)
FROG: 1 3" square origami (green, colored on both sides)
Note See P.7 for "RING" instructions.

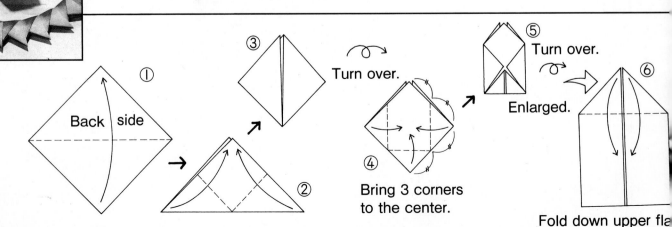

① Back side

②

③ Turn over.

④ Bring 3 corners to the center.

⑤ Turn over.
Enlarged.

⑥ Fold down upper fla

#6 TWO-TONE RING WITH GOLDFISH (P.7)

Completed size 5" diameter

Materials RING: 50 1½"×3" rectangles of origami paper (gradated color)
GOLDFISH: 1 3" square origami (red, colored on both sides)
Note See P.7 for "RING" instructions.

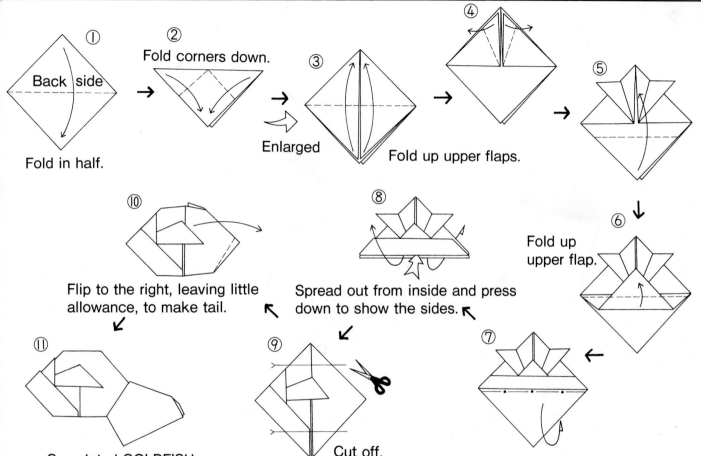

① Back side
Fold in half.

② Fold corners down.

Enlarged

③ Fold up upper flaps.

④

⑤

⑥ Fold up upper flap.

⑦ Fold back.

⑧ Spread out from inside and press down to show the sides.

⑨ Cut off.

⑩ Flip to the right, leaving little allowance, to make tail.

⑪ Completed GOLDFISH.

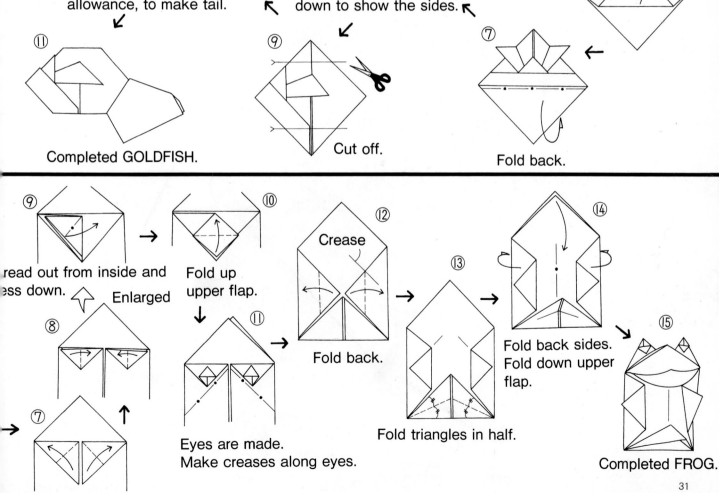

⑨ read out from inside and ess down.

Enlarged

⑧

⑦

⑩ Fold up upper flap.

⑪ Eyes are made. Make creases along eyes.

⑫ Crease
Fold back.

⑬ Fold triangles in half.

⑭ Fold back sides. Fold down upper flap.

⑮ Completed FROG.

Materials #2: 12 3"×6" rectangles of origami paper (gradated color)
#3: 12 4¾"×9½" rectangles of origami paper (6 colors)
Note The completed project may look different depending on the thickness of the paper used.

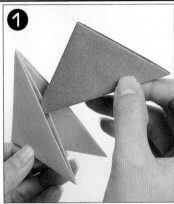

❶ Holding the first piece double pocket facing left, insert the points of the second piece into the longer pockets, not too deeply.

❷ Insert the third piece into the second.

❸ Insert the fourth piece into the third.

❹ Insert the points of the first piece into the fourth.

❺ Push the corners inward to make table top.

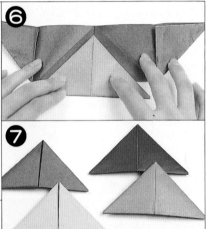

❻

Make legs. Unfold a triangular piece. Place another unfolded piece in the center.

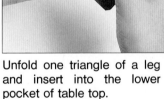

❼

Fold again to make reinforced leg. Make 4.

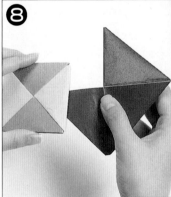

❽ Unfold one triangle of a leg and insert into the lower pocket of table top.

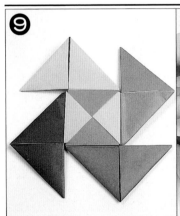

❾ Repeat with the remaining legs.

❿ Bring the triangular flap onto the "table top". Repeat with remaining legs.

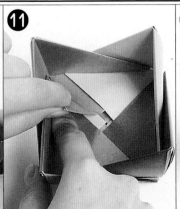

⓫ Insert the final flap under the first triangle.

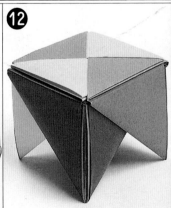

⓬ Completed ORNAMENT STAND.

32

#7 & #8 CHRISTMAS TREE (P.7)

Completed size
#7: 5" high
#8: 4" high

Materials #7: 9 3"×6" rectangles of origami paper (dark green)
　　　　　　1 3"×6" rectangle of origami paper (browm)
　　　　#8: 5 3"×6" rectangles of origami paper (green)
　　　　　　1 3"×6" rectangle of origami paper (brown)
　　　　　　11 sequins and beads

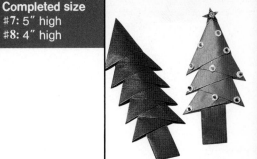

Make trunk.

See left, ① to ⑥.

Fold in half.

Inserting points

Make triangles for leaves.

① Back side
Fold in half.

② Fold in half again.

③ Fold up corner.

④

⑤ Fold up corner.

Turn over.

⑥ Open.

⑦ Fold corners in.

Tuck in corner.

⑧ Leave a little space.

⑨ Fold in half.
⅛" difference.

⑩ Completed piece
Duoble pocket

9 pcs. are used for FIR TREE.

Trunk

FIR TREE

Glue on sequins and beads.

5 pcs. are used for TREE WITH LIGHTS.

Trunk

TREE WITH LIGHTS

Double pocket

Insert and glue.

Double pocket

Double pocket

Double pocket

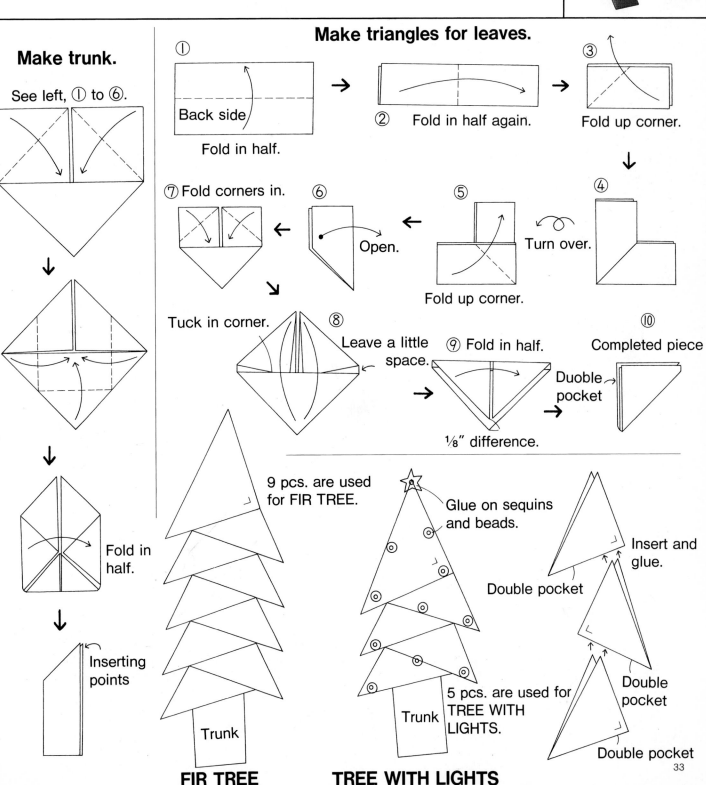

33

#16–#19 GOLDFISH (P.10)

Completed size #16 & #17: 2″ wide, 5″ long #18 & #19: 1⅛″ wide, 3⅛″ long
Materials #16: 16 3″×6″ rectangles of origami paper (gradated color)
                12 3″×6″ rectangles of origami paper (solid)
         #17: 28 3″×6″ rectangles of origami paper (assorted colors)
         #18 & #19: 28 1¾″×3¾″ rectangles of glossy paper (from magazine)
         2 ¼″ diam. plastic eyes each
*See opposite page for diagram.

❶

Hold the first piece double pocket facing the left, and insert its points into the adjoining pockets of two pcs. to form Row 2.

❷

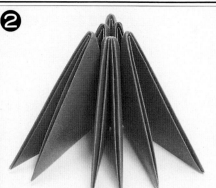

Insert into 3 pcs. to make Row 3.

❸

Join 4 pcs. as Row 4, then 5 pcs. as Row 5.

❹

Join 4 pcs. as Row 6. Open side triangles of Row 5 to form fins.

❺

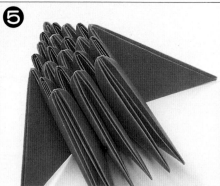

Join 3 pcs. as Row 7. Insert side flaps of Row 6 into the outer pockets.

❻

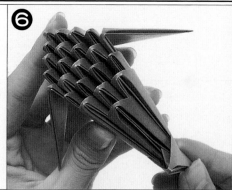

Insert the center 4 points into 1 pc. to form Row 8.

❼

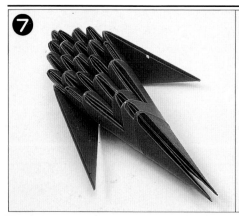

Insert all points into 1 pc. Repeat Row 10 so the tail tapers.

❽

Make tail fin: Join 2 pcs. to make Row 11, and 1 pc. for Row 12.

❾

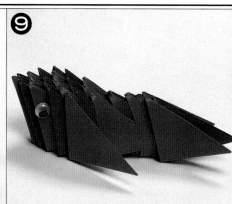

Glue on eyes to finish.

34

#28-#30 TOOTHPICK HOLDER (P.15)

Completed size #28 & #30: 2″ high, 1¾″ wide #29: 2½″ high, 2″ wide
Materials #28: 64 1½″×3″ rectangles of patterned *washi* paper
  5 1½″×3″ rectangles of solid *washi* paper
 #29: 69 1¾″×3¾″ rectangles of glossy paper (from magazine)
 #30: 69 1½″×3″ rectangles of patterned *washi* paper
Note The completed project may look different depending on the thickness of the paper used.

#16 – #19
GOLDFISH & FISH

Tail { ▽ ·········· Row 12 (1 pc.)
  ▽ ▽ ·········· Row 11 (2 pcs.)
  ▽ ·········· Row 10 (1 pc.)
  ▽ ·········· Row 9 (1 pc.)
  ▽ ·········· Row 8 (1 pc.)
  ▽ ▽ ▽ ·········· Row 7 (3 pcs.)
Fin ▽ ▽ ▽ ▽ ·········· Row 6 (4 pcs.)
  ▽ ▽ ▽ ▽ ▽ ·········· Row 5 (5 pcs.)
  ▽ ▽ ▽ ▽ ·········· Row 4 (4 pcs.)
Eye attaching position ▽ ▽ ▽ ·········· Row 3 (3 pcs.)
  ▽ ▽ ·········· Row 2 (2 pcs.)
  ▽ ·········· Row 1 (1 pc.)

#28 – #30 TOOTHPICK HOLDER

Handle (5 pcs.) { ▽ ▽ ▽ ▽ ▽

▽▽▽▽▽▽▽▽▽▽▽▽▽ ·········· Row 5
▽▽▽▽▽▽▽▽▽▽▽▽▽ ·········· Row 4   13 pcs. in each row.
▽▽▽▽▽▽▽▽▽▽▽▽▽ ·········· Row 3
▽▽▽▽▽▽▽▽▽▽▽▽▽ ·········· Row 2
△△△△△△△△△△△△△ ·········· Row 1

Join ends to form a ring of 13 pcs.

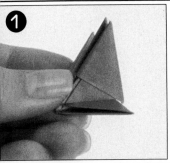

❶ Hold a pair of pieces, double pockets down and the right angles away from you. Join them with a piece, the right angle facing you. Repeat to make 6 3-pc sets.

❷ Join all sets by inserting adjoining points into a new piece.

❸ Join into a ring. 13 pcs. are used for Row 1.

❹ Rows 3-5: Join in the same direction. The center of bottom is somewhat twisted.

❺ Insert any 2 adjoining points into a piece of handle.

❻ Secure handle with glue.

35

#20 SOARING CRANE (P.10)

Materials

53 3″×6″ rectangles of origami paper (white)
15 3″×6″ rectangles of origami paper (black)
16 2″×3½″ rectangles of origami paper (white)
 1 2″×3½″ rectangle of origami paper (red)
 2 ¼″ diam. plastic eyes

Note

The completed project may look different depending on the thickness of the paper used.

Head/Neck

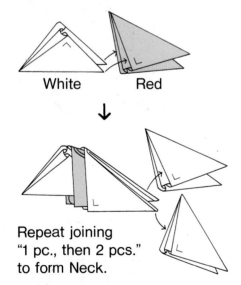

White   Red

↓

Repeat joining "1 pc., then 2 pcs." to form Neck.

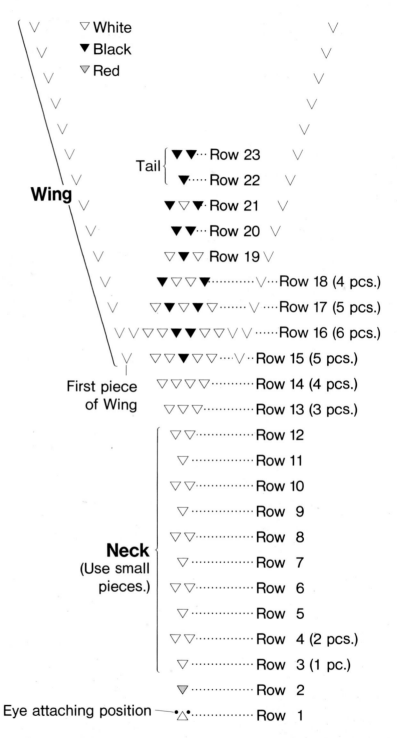

Wing

∇ White
▼ Black
▽ Red

Tail {
▼ ▼··· Row 23
▼···· Row 22
}

▼ ▽ ▼· Row 21
▼ ▼··· Row 20
▽ ▼ ▽ Row 19
▼ ▽ ▽ ▼··········∨···Row 18 (4 pcs.)
▽ ▼ ▽ ▼ ▽····· ∨···Row 17 (5 pcs.)
∨∨∨∨▼▼▼▽▽∨∨·····Row 16 (6 pcs.)
▽▽▼▽▽···∨·Row 15 (5 pcs.)

First piece of Wing

▽▽▽▽········Row 14 (4 pcs.)
▽▽▽········Row 13 (3 pcs.)

Neck
(Use small pieces.)

▽▽···········Row 12
▽············Row 11
▽▽···········Row 10
▽············Row 9
▽▽···········Row 8
▽············Row 7
▽▽···········Row 6
▽············Row 5
▽▽············Row 4 (2 pcs.)
▽············Row 3 (1 pc.)
▽············Row 2

Eye attaching position ─•△•············ Row 1

Signs for piece direction

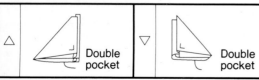

| △ | Double pocket | ▽ | Double pocket | ∧ | Double pocket | ∨ | Double pocket | ↓ | Insert here. |

❶
Using smaller pieces, make beak and head referring to the opposite page.

❷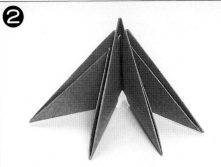
Holding a white piece in the same direction, join to the red. (Side view)

❸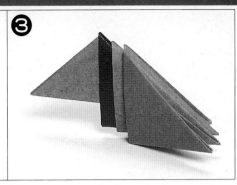
Join 2 pcs. to make Row 4.

❹
Repeat (1 pc.−2 pcs.) until Row 12 is done. Neck part is completed.

❺
Insert end flaps into 3 pcs. to make Row 13.

❻
Join 4 pcs. as Row 14.

❼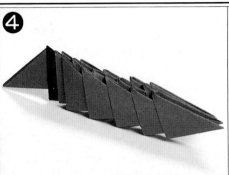
Rows 5-23: Check the number and color of pieces with the diagram shown left.

❽
Row 21 is completed.

❾
Row 22: Join 1 black pc. Row 23: Join 2 black pcs. Tail is completed.

❿
Make wing. Referring to diagram on P.38, insert 1 basic piece into 2 pcs. Then join 1 pc. to one side, inserting the point into outer pocket. Repeat until 14 pcs. are joined. Make a pair.

⓫
Insert into Row 16 of the body.

⓬
Glue on eyes to finish.

Completed size
6¼" wide, 5" long

Materials 〈#21〉 [#22]
30 3"×6" rectangles of origami paper 〈green〉 [blue]
2 3"×6" rectangles of origami paper 〈orange〉 [orange]
1 2"×3½" rectangle of origami paper 〈black〉 [yellow]
19 3"×6" rectangles of craft paper 〈patterned〉 [patterned]
2 ¼" diam. plastic eyes each

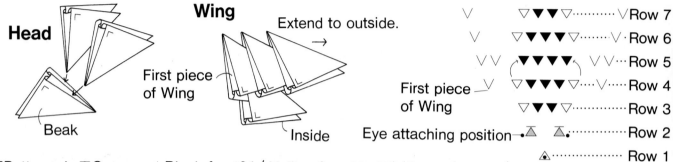

Head

Beak

Wing

Extend to outside.

First piece of Wing

Inside

▼······ Row 13
▼······ Row 12
∨   ▼······ Row 11   ∨
∨   ▼······ Row 10   ∨
∨   ▽▽···· Row 9 ∨
∨   ▽▼▽·· Row 8 ∨
∨   ▽▼▼▽·········· ∨ Row 7
∨   ▽▼▼▼▽······· ∨· Row 6
∨∨   (▼▼▼▼) ∨∨··· Row 5
First piece ∨ ▽▼▼▼▽···· ∨···· Row 4
of Wing   ▽▼▼▼▽·········· Row 3
Eye attaching position →△ △.·············· Row 2
△·············· Row 1

▼Patterned △Orange ▲Black for #21/ Yellow for #22 ▽∨Green for #21/ Blue for #22

❶

Make head referring to the figure above. Insert 2 pcs. into 1 pc.

❷

Row 3: Join 2 origami pcs. and 2 patterned pcs.

❸

Row 4: Join 3 origami pcs. and 2 patterned pcs. Row 5: Join 4 origami pcs. covering the side flaps of previous row.

❹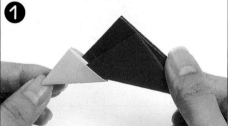

Work on Rows 5-9, as directed in the diagram.

❺

Make tail. Join 1 pc. on each row; repeat 3 times.

❻

Make wing. Insert 1 basic pc. into 2 pcs. Join 1 pc. only to one side, inserting the point into outer pocket. Join 6 pcs. to the same side. Make 2.

❼

Insert the base of wing into Row 6 of the body.

❽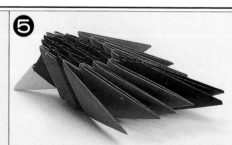

Attach the other wing. Glue on eyes.

❾

Completed KINGFISHER.

#23 SWALLOW (P.11)

Completed size
6″ wide, 6″ long

Materials
61 3″×6″ rectangles of origami paper (black)
24 3″×6″ rectangles of origami paper (gradated gray)
2 ¼″ diam. plastic eyes

Note
The completed project may look different depending on the thickness of the paper used.

▼▽ Black
▽ Gray

Row

▼▼ ······· 20
▼▼ ······· 19
▼▼ ······· 18
▼▼ ······· 17
▼▼ ······· 16   Join 1 pc.
▼▼ ······· 15   each for
▼▼ ······· 14   separate Tail.

Tail

▼   ▼ ······· 13   ▼
▼   ▼ ······· 12   ▼
▼   ▼ ······· 11   ▼
▼   ▽▽ ······· 10   ▼
▼   ▽▽▽ ······· 9   ▼
▼   ▽▽▽▽ ······· 8   ▼
▼   ▼▽▽▽▽▼··· 7   ▼
▽ ▽▼▽▽▽▼▽ ·········▽· Row 6
▽ ▽▼▽▽▽▼▽ ·········▽· Row 5
▽ ▽ ▽▽▽▽ ····▽····▽···· Row 4
▽▽ ▽▽▽ ·······▽▽ ······ Row 3
First ▽ •▼▼• ········▽· Row 2
piece of ▲▲ ················· Row 1
Wing   Eye attaching position

Head

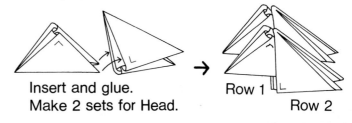

Insert and glue.
Make 2 sets for Head.

→

Row 1   Row 2

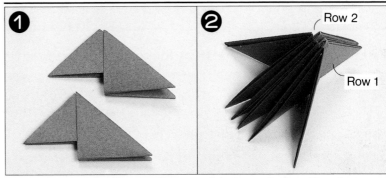

❶ Make head referring to figure above. Make 2 sets.

❷ Join 3 pcs. to form Row 3.   Row 2   Row 1

❸ Rows 4-7: Work as directed above. Row 8: Join by covering side flaps of previous row.

❹ Row 10 is done.

❺ Make tail base by joining 1 pc. in the next 3 rows.

❻ Split the tail and join 1 pc. each in Row 7.

❼ Make wing. Insert 1 basic piece into 2 pcs. Join 1 pc. only to one side for Row 4, inserting the point into outer pocket. Join 1 pc. covering previous row in Row 8.

❽ Make 2 wings. Join by inserting side flap of Row 5 into the wing.

❾ Attach eyes to finish.

39

#26 & #27 BASKET (P.14)

Materials (for each item)
163 2¾" × 6" rectangles of patterned paper
Note
The completed project may look different depending on the thickness of the paper used.

＊Basket and hat are made in a similar way. The procedure is the same until Step 5, on the opposite pa

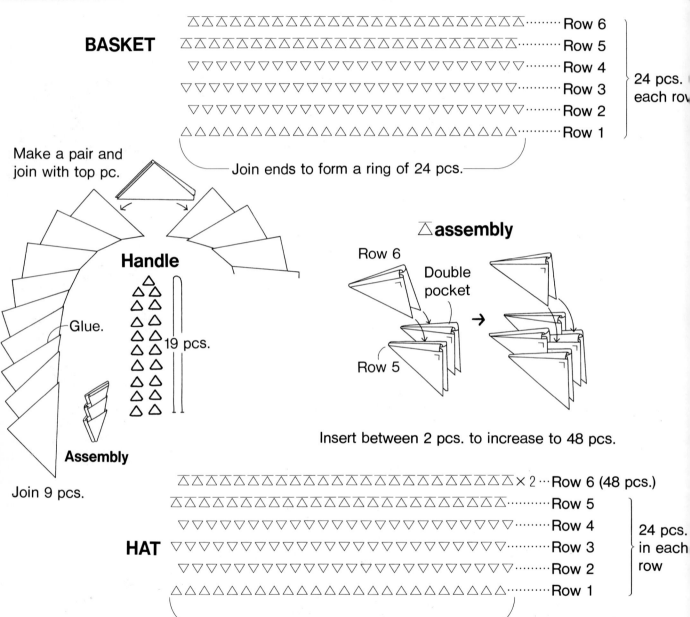

BASKET

△△△△△△△△△△△△△△△△△△△△△△△ ······· Row 6
△△△△△△△△△△△△△△△△△△△△△△△ ······· Row 5
▽▽▽▽▽▽▽▽▽▽▽▽▽▽▽▽▽▽▽▽▽▽▽▽ ······· Row 4
▽▽▽▽▽▽▽▽▽▽▽▽▽▽▽▽▽▽▽▽▽▽▽▽ ······· Row 3
▽▽▽▽▽▽▽▽▽▽▽▽▽▽▽▽▽▽▽▽▽▽▽▽ ······· Row 2
△△△△△△△△△△△△△△△△△△△△△△△ ······· Row 1

} 24 pcs. each row

Make a pair and join with top pc.

Join ends to form a ring of 24 pcs.

Handle

△△△
△△△
△△△
△△
△△ 19 pcs.
△△
△△
△△
△△
△△

Glue.

Assembly

Join 9 pcs.

△ **assembly**

Row 6

Double pocket

Row 5

→

Insert between 2 pcs. to increase to 48 pcs.

△△△△△△△△△△△△△△△△△△△△△△△ × 2 ··· Row 6 (48 pcs.)
△△△△△△△△△△△△△△△△△△△△△△△ ········· Row 5
▽▽▽▽▽▽▽▽▽▽▽▽▽▽▽▽▽▽▽▽▽▽▽▽ ········· Row 4
HAT ▽▽▽▽▽▽▽▽▽▽▽▽▽▽▽▽▽▽▽▽▽▽▽▽ ········· Row 3
▽▽▽▽▽▽▽▽▽▽▽▽▽▽▽▽▽▽▽▽▽▽▽▽ ········· Row 2
△△△△△△△△△△△△△△△△△△△△△△△ ········· Row 1

} 24 pcs. in each row

Join ends to form a ring of 24 pcs.

Signs for piece direction

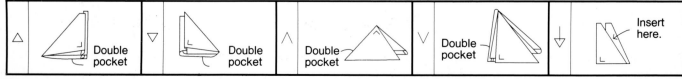

| △ Double pocket | ▽ Double pocket | ∧ Double pocket | ∨ Double pocket | ⤓ Insert here. |

#31–#33 HAT (p.15)

Completed size
#31 & #32: 6¼" wide, 3⅛" high
#33: 3½" wide, 2" high

Materials
#31: 168 3"×6" rectangles of origami paper (blue)
#32: 168 3"×6" rectangles of origami pape (balck)
#33: 168 1¾"×3¾" rectangles of glossy paper (from magazine)

Note
The completed project may look different depending on the thickness of the paper used.

❶ Apply glue onto tips and join 6 pcs. Make 4 sets.

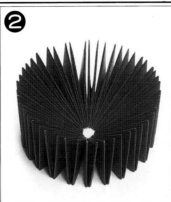

❷ Join into a ring by gluing points.

❸ Insert each 24 pcs. for Rows 2-4.

❹ Join Row 5 by holding a piece double pocket facing up and the right angle facing in.

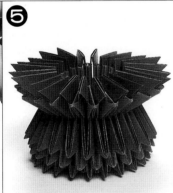

❺ Work Row 6 in the same manner. (Proceed to Step ❽ for HAT.)

❻ Make handle referring to the figure on the opposite page.

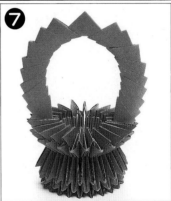

❼ Insert ends of handle into BASKET and glue to secure.

❽ **HAT ASSEMBLY**

Fill between pieces by inserting 1 pc., all around.

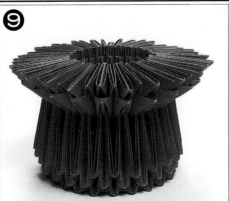

❾ Check the shape and glue several hidden points to secure.

❿ Tie ribbon around to finish.

Completed size
#34: 5" wide, 6¾" high
#35: 4½" wide, 5½" high

Materials
#34: 375 2¾"×6⅜" rectangles of patterned paper (green)
#35: 375 2¾"×6⅜" rectangles of patterned paper (orange)
1 20"×12" crepe paper (green)
7 14" #28 wrapped wire (green)
4" 1/12" thick craft wire
60" ½" floral tape
＊Materials except rectangular paper are for each item.

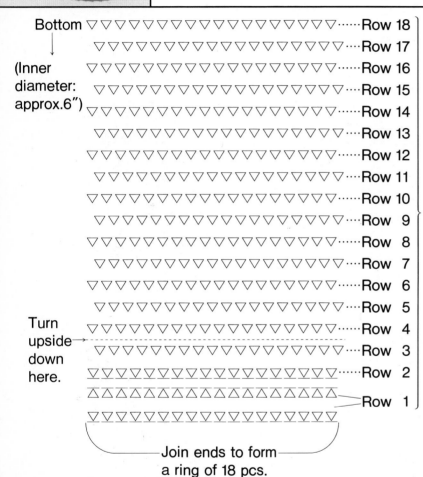

Bottom ▽▽▽▽▽▽▽▽▽▽▽▽▽▽▽▽▽▽······Row 18
▽▽▽▽▽▽▽▽▽▽▽▽▽▽▽▽▽·····Row 17
(Inner diameter: approx.6") ▽▽▽▽▽▽▽▽▽▽▽▽▽▽▽▽▽▽······Row 16
▽▽▽▽▽▽▽▽▽▽▽▽▽▽▽▽▽·····Row 15
▽▽▽▽▽▽▽▽▽▽▽▽▽▽▽▽▽▽······Row 14
▽▽▽▽▽▽▽▽▽▽▽▽▽▽▽▽▽·····Row 13
▽▽▽▽▽▽▽▽▽▽▽▽▽▽▽▽▽▽····Row 12
▽▽▽▽▽▽▽▽▽▽▽▽▽▽▽▽▽·····Row 11
▽▽▽▽▽▽▽▽▽▽▽▽▽▽▽▽▽▽·····Row 10
▽▽▽▽▽▽▽▽▽▽▽▽▽▽▽▽▽·····Row 9
▽▽▽▽▽▽▽▽▽▽▽▽▽▽▽▽▽▽····Row 8
▽▽▽▽▽▽▽▽▽▽▽▽▽▽▽▽▽·····Row 7
▽▽▽▽▽▽▽▽▽▽▽▽▽▽▽▽▽▽·····Row 6
▽▽▽▽▽▽▽▽▽▽▽▽▽▽▽▽▽·····Row 5
Turn upside down here. →▽▽▽▽▽▽▽▽▽▽▽▽▽▽▽▽▽▽·····Row 4
▽▽▽▽▽▽▽▽▽▽▽▽▽▽▽▽▽·····Row 3
▽▽▽▽▽▽▽▽▽▽▽▽▽▽▽▽▽▽·····Row 2
△△△△△△△△△△△△△△△△△△⟵Row 1
▽▽▽▽▽▽▽▽▽▽▽▽▽▽▽▽▽▽

Fruit
18 pcs. in each row

Join ends to form a ring of 18 pcs.

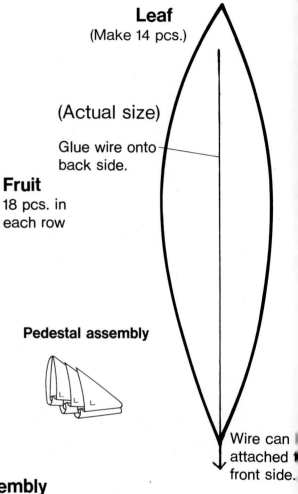

Leaf
(Make 14 pcs.)

(Actual size)

Glue wire onto back side.

Pedestal assembly

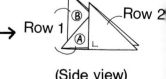
L L L

Wire can attached front side.

Row 1 to Row 2 assembly

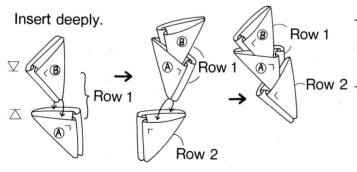

Insert deeply.

▽
ⓑ
△
}Row 1
ⓐ

→

ⓑ
ⓐ Row 1
Row 2

→

ⓑ ⟵Row 1
ⓐ
Row 2

Make 18 sets.
Be sure to interlock securely.

→

ⓑ Row 2
Row 1
ⓐ

(Side view)

↓

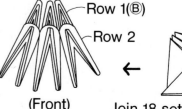

Row 1(ⓑ)
Row 2

(Front)

←

L

Join 18 sets to form a ring.
(See Step 2, opposite page.)

❶

Referring to the figures on the opposite page, join 3 pcs. and glue to secure. Make 18 sets.

❷

Join 2 sets by inserting their adjoining points into a new piece. Continue to form a ring.

❸

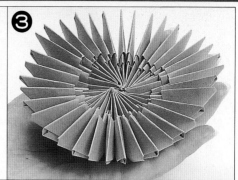

Turn over and hold in your hand.

❹

For Row 4 to Row 18, join the pieces at an angle to form a pineapple shape.

❺

Row 18 is completed.

❻

Turn upside down so the 1st row comes on top.

❼

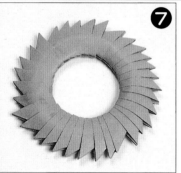

Make pedestal referring to the diagram on the opposite page.

❽

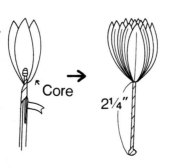

Form leaves as illustrated below.

Core Direction of creases

½″

6¾″–7″

Cut out 14 leaves from crepe paper.

Glue wrapped wire onto back side.

Cover top ½″ with floral tape.

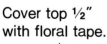

Craft wire (2¾″–3″)

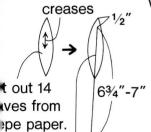

Core

2¼″

❾

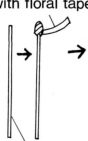

Insert stem into the top and place on the pedestal.

Using floral tape, attach leaves around wire, 2-3 pcs. at a time.
Add 2-3 leaves binding with floral tape. Repeat until all leaves are attached. Bind down the tape and make a lump at the end. Insert into the top of the fruit. Arrange leaves attractively.

43

#36 & #37 MINI PINEAPPLE (P.16)

Completed size
#36: 2" wide, 2⅜" high
#37: 2¼" wide, 2¾" high

Materials
#36: 118 1½"×3" rectangles of origami paper (yellow)
26 1½"×3" rectangles of origami paper (green)
12 1½"×3" rectangles of origami paper (brown)
#37: 123 1½"×3" rectangles of origami paper (yellow, 4 colors)
28 1½"×3" rectangles of origami paper (green)
21 1½"×3" rectangles of origami paper (brown)
10 1½"×3" rectangles of origami paper (pale green)

#37
▽ Yellow
▼ Brown
▽ Pale green

#36
▽ Yellow
▼ Brown

#37

Leaves (2 rows)
······ Row 11
····· Row 10
····· Row 9
····· Row 8
····· Row 7
····· Row 6
····· Row 5
····· Row 4
····· Row 3
····· Row 2
······ Row 1

14 pcs. in each row.

Join ends to form a ring of 14 pcs.

#36

Leaves (2 rows)
······· Row 10
······· Row 9
······· Row 8
········ Row 7
······· Row 6
······· Row 5
······· Row 4
······· Row 3
······· Row 2
········ Row 1

13 pcs in each row.

Join ends to form a ring of 13 pcs.

Signs of direction

Leaf assembly

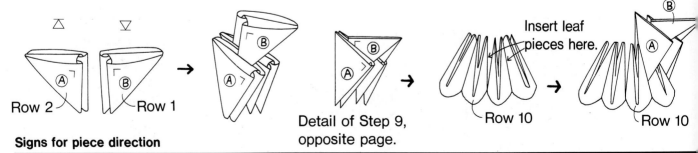

Row 2 Ⓐ Ⓑ Row 1

Detail of Step 9, opposite page.

Insert leaf pieces here.

Ⓑ Ⓐ

Row 10

Row 10

Signs for piece direction

| △ | Double pocket | ▽ | Double pocket | ∧ | Double pocket | ∨ | Double pocket | ↓ | Insert here. |

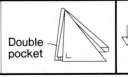

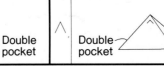

❶

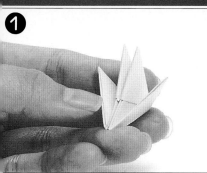

Hold a pair of pieces, double pockets down and the right angles away from you. Join them with a piece, right angle facing you.

❷

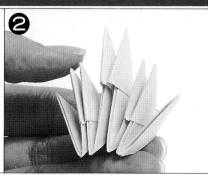

Make another set, and join them with 1 piece.

❸

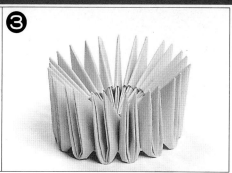

Repeat and join into a ring. The center of bottom can look somewhat twisted.

❹

Row 3: Insert yellow and brown pieces alternately, all around.

❺

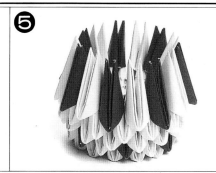

Rows 4-5: Join yellow pcs. all around.
Row 6: Work the same as Row 3.

❻

Row 7: Join yellow pcs. all around.
Row 8: Join yellow pcs., plus one pale green.

❼

Row 9: Work the same as Row 2.

❽

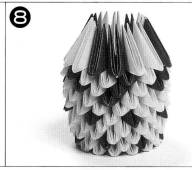

Rows 10-11: Work as directed in the diagram shown on the opposite page.

❾

Make top: Interlock 3 green pcs. as shown on the opposite page. Make 7 sets.

❿

Insert each set of leaves into the fruit as shown on the opposite page.

⓫

Join 2 adjacent sets by inserting a new piece all around.

⓬

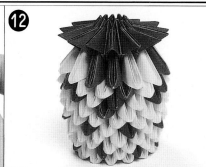

Check the shape of leaves and glue to secure.

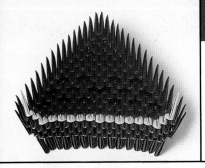

Completed size
4″ wide, 4¾″ long

Materials 114 1½″×3″ rectangles of origami paper (red)
66 1½″×3″ rectangles of origami paper (green)
17 1½″×3″ rectangles of origami paper (white)
16 1½″×3″ rectangles of origami paper (black)
Note The completed project may look different depending on the thickness of the paper used

❶

Hold 1 pc. so double pocket faces right. Apply some glue onto points of another piece and insert into the pockets.

❷
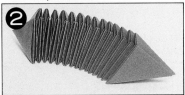
Repeat until Row 1 and 2 are constructed.

❸

Row 3: Join 15 pcs., tucking in side flaps of the bottom row.

❹

Join Rows 2 and 3 as directed. (Turn upside down)

❺

Work Row 5 by changing colors as directed in the diagram, and add 1 green pc. to each side.

❻

Row 6: Work as directed.
Row 7: Work with white and red.
Row 8: Work with red and black.

❼
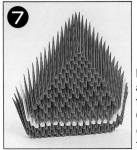
Rows 9-21: Work as directed in the diagram. Glue green flaps each other to finish.

▽ Red
▼ Black
▽ White
▽ Green

▽ .... Row 21 (1 pc.)
▽ ▽ .... Row 20 (2 pcs.)
▽ ▽ ▽ .... Row 19 (3 pcs.)
▽ ▽ ▽ ▽ .... Row 18 (4 pcs.)
▽ ▽ ▽ ▽ ▽ .... Row 17 (5 pcs.)
▽ ▽ ▽ ▽ ▽ ▽ .... Row 16 (6 pcs.)
▽ ▽ ▽ ▽ ▽ ▽ ▽ .... Row 15 (7 pcs.)
▽ ▽ ▽ ▽ ▽ ▽ ▽ ▽ .... Row 14 (8 pcs.)
▽ ▽ ▽ ▽ ▽ ▽ ▽ ▽ ▽ .... Row 13 (9 pcs.)
▽ ▼ ▽ ▼ ▽ ▽ ▼ ▽ ▼ ▽ .... Row 12 (10 pcs.)
▽ ▽ ▽ ▽ ▽ ▽ ▽ ▽ ▽ ▽ ▽ .... Row 11 (11 pcs.)
▽ ▼ ▽ ▼ ▽ ▼ ▼ ▽ ▼ ▽ ▼ ▽ .... Row 10 (12 pcs.)
▽ ▽ ▽ ▽ ▽ ▽ ▽ ▽ ▽ ▽ ▽ ▽ ▽ .... Row 9 (13 pcs.)
▽ ▼ ▽ ▼ ▼ ▽ ▼ ▼ ▽ ▼ ▼ ▽ ▼ ▽ .... Row 8 (14 pcs.)
▽ ▽ ▽ ▽ ▽ ▽ ▽ ▽ ▽ ▽ ▽ ▽ ▽ ▽ ▽ .... Row 7 (15 pcs.)
▽ ▽ ▽ ▽ ▽ ▽ ▽ ▽ ▽ ▽ ▽ ▽ ▽ ▽ ▽ ▽ .... Row 6 (16 pcs.)
Green — ▽ ▽ ▽ ▽ ▽ ▽ ▽ ▽ ▽ ▽ ▽ ▽ ▽ ▽ ▽ ▽ ▽ .... Row 5 (15＋2 pcs.) — Green
▽ ▽ ▽ ▽ ▽ ▽ ▽ ▽ ▽ ▽ ▽ ▽ ▽ ▽ ▽ ▽ .... Row 4 (16 pcs.)
▽ ▽ ▽ ▽ ▽ ▽ ▽ ▽ ▽ ▽ ▽ ▽ ▽ ▽ ▽ .... Row 3 (15 pcs.)
▽ ▽ ▽ ▽ ▽ ▽ ▽ ▽ ▽ ▽ ▽ ▽ ▽ ▽ .... Row 2 (14 pcs.)
△ △ △ △ △ △ △ △ △ △ △ △ △ △ △ .... Row 1 (15 pcs.)

Join ends to form
a ring of 15 pcs.

#40 STRAWBERRY (P.17)

Completed size
1¾" wide, 2" long

Materials (for 3 strawberries)
90 1½×3" rectangles of origami paper (red)
18 1½"×3" rectangles of origami paper (green)
18 black beads
Note
The completed project may look different depending on the thickness of the paper used.

▽ Red
▼ Green
● Bead attaching position

▽·············Row 10 (1 pc.)
●
▽ ▽·············Row 9 (2 pcs.)
▽ ▽ ▽···········Row 8 (3 pcs.)
● ●
▽ ▽ ▽ ▽·········Row 7 (4 pcs.)
▽ ▽ ▽ ▽ ▽·······Row 6 (5 pcs.)
● ●
▽ ▽ ▽ ▽ ▽ ▽······Row 5 (6 pcs.)
▽ ▽ ▽ ▽ ▽·······Row 4 (5 pcs.)
●
▽ ▽ ▽ ▽ ▽·······Row 3 (4 pcs.)

Green
▼·············Row 2 Green
▼ ···········Row 1

❶

Holding 2 green pcs., double folds down, and insert one into the other.

❷

Insert points of green into double pockets of 2 red pcs. Place 1 pc. on each side.

❸

Join them with 5 pcs. to complete Row 5.

❹

Join 6 pcs. to complete Row 6.

❺

Row 7: Join 5 pcs.
Row 7: Join 4 pcs.

❻

Row 8: Join 3 pcs.

❼

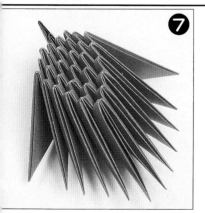

Row 9: Join 2 pcs. Row 10: Join 1 pc.

❽

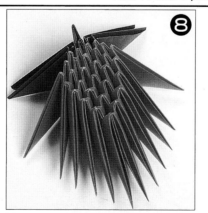

Make top: Insert a point of green piece into Row 3. Add 3 more green pcs.

❾

Glue on black beads to finish.

＊Pieces used in the actual project are smaller.   47

Materials
#41: 388 1″×2″ rectangles of origami paper (gold *washi*)
        4 1″×2″ rectangles of origami paper (silver *washi*)
#42: 329 1½″×3″ rectangles of origami paper (gradated red *washi*)
        62 1½″×3″ rectangles of origami paper (gold *washi*)
          1 1½″×3″ rectangle of origami paper (silver *washi*)

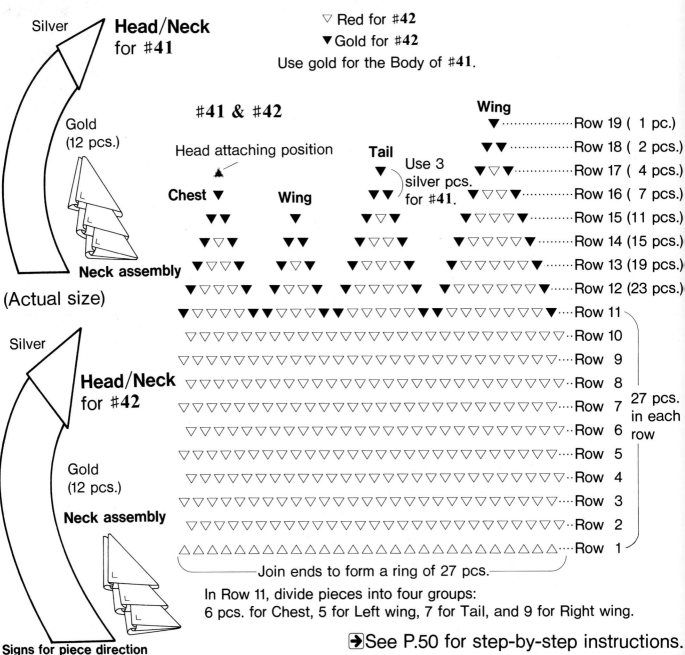

Silver

Head/Neck
for #41

▽ Red for #42
▼ Gold for #42
Use gold for the Body of #41.

Gold
(12 pcs.)

#41 & #42

Head attaching position

Wing
▼ ·············· Row 19 (1 pc.)
▼ ▼ ·············· Row 18 (2 pcs.)

Tail
▼   Use 3
▼ ▼   silver pcs.
             for #41.

Chest ▼   **Wing**   ▼ ▽ ▼ ·············· Row 17 (4 pcs.)
▼ ▼   ▼   ▼ ▽ ▽ ▼ ·············· Row 16 (7 pcs.)
▼ ▽ ▼   ▼ ▼   ▼ ▽ ▼   ▼ ▽ ▽ ▽ ▼ ·············· Row 15 (11 pcs.)
▼ ▽ ▽ ▼   ▼ ▼   ▼ ▽ ▼   ▼ ▽ ▽ ▽ ▼ ·············· Row 14 (15 pcs.)

Neck assembly   ▼ ▽ ▽ ▽ ▼   ▼ ▽ ▽ ▼   ▼ ▽ ▽ ▽ ▼   ▼ ▽ ▽ ▽ ▽ ▼ ·· Row 13 (19 pcs.)
▼ ▽ ▽ ▽ ▽ ▼ ▼ ▽ ▽ ▽ ▼ ▼ ▽ ▽ ▽ ▽ ▼ ▼ ▽ ▽ ▽ ▽ ▽ ▼ ···· Row 12 (23 pcs.)

(Actual size)

▼ ▽ ▽ ▽ ▽ ▽ ▽ ▽ ▼ ▼ ▽ ▽ ▽ ▼ ▼ ▽ ▽ ▽ ▽ ▼ ▼ ▽ ▽ ▽ ▽ ▽ ▼ ···· Row 11

Silver

▽ ···· Row 10
▽ ···· Row 9

Head/Neck
for #42

▽ ···· Row 8
▽ ···· Row 7   27 pcs.
▽ ···· Row 6   in each
row
Gold
(12 pcs.)

▽ ···· Row 5
▽ ···· Row 4

Neck assembly

▽ ···· Row 3
▽ ···· Row 2
△ ···· Row 1

└── Join ends to form a ring of 27 pcs. ──┘

In Row 11, divide pieces into four groups:
6 pcs. for Chest, 5 for Left wing, 7 for Tail, and 9 for Right wing.

➡See P.50 for step-by-step instructions.

Signs for piece direction

| △ | Double pocket | ▽ | Double pocket | ∧ | Double pocket | ∨ | Double pocket | ↓ | Insert here. |

#43: 60 1¾″×3½″ rectangles of *washi* paper (red)
    79 1¾″×3½″ rectangles of *washi* paper (green)
    75 1¾″×3½″ rectangles of *washi* paper (purple)
    74 1¾″×3½″ rectangles of *washi* paper (blue)
    4 1¾″×3½″ rectangles of *washi* paper (gold)

Note
The completed project may look different depending on the thickness of the paper used.

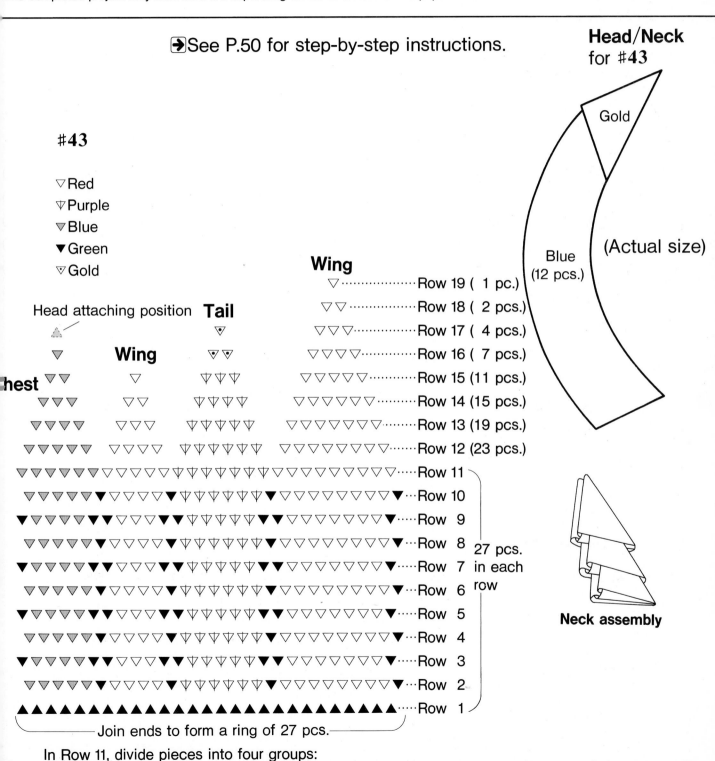

➡See P.50 for step-by-step instructions.

Head/Neck
for #43

Gold

#43

▽ Red
▽ Purple
▽ Blue
▼ Green
▽ Gold

(Actual size)

Blue
(12 pcs.)

Wing
▽ ················· Row 19 (1 pc.)
▽▽ ················· Row 18 (2 pcs.)
▽▽▽ ················· Row 17 (4 pcs.)
▽▽▽▽ ················· Row 16 (7 pcs.)
▽▽▽▽▽ ················· Row 15 (11 pcs.)
▽▽▽▽▽▽ ················· Row 14 (15 pcs.)
▽▽▽▽▽▽▽ ················· Row 13 (19 pcs.)
▽▽▽▽▽▽▽ ················· Row 12 (23 pcs.)

Head attaching position **Tail**
Chest **Wing**

Row 11
Row 10
Row 9
Row 8   27 pcs.
Row 7   in each
Row 6   row
Row 5
Row 4
Row 3
Row 2
········· Row 1

Join ends to form a ring of 27 pcs.

Neck assembly

In Row 11, divide pieces into four groups:
6 pcs. for Chest, 5 for Left wing, 7 for Tail, and 9 for Right wing.

49

❶ Holding pieces double pockets down, interlock vertically, alternating the direction of the right angle, until 27 pcs. are joined.

❷ Row 3: Cover adjoining points of Row 2 with 1 pc.

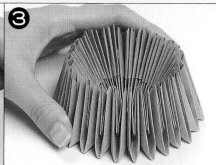

❸ Continue all around to make a circle of 27 pcs. (See diagram on the previous page for color layout.)

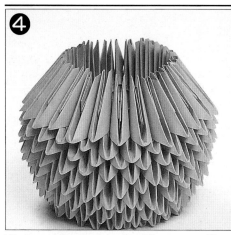

❹ Work as directed in the diagram until 11 rows are done.

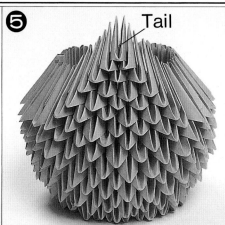

❺ Tail

Divide pieces into chest(6), left wing(5), tail(7) and right wing(9). Work on tail part as directed.

❻ Left wing

Then work on the left wing.

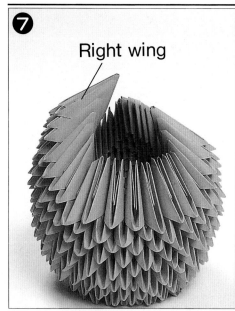

❼ Right wing

Work on the right wing.

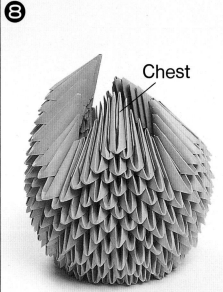

❽ Chest

Work on the chest.

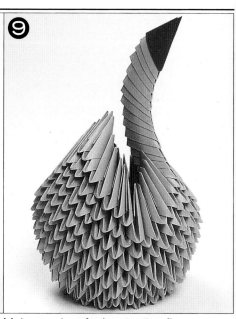

❾ Make neck referring to the figure on the previous page, and insert into the top of chest.

✳Pieces used in the actual project are smaller.

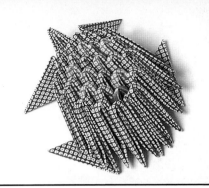

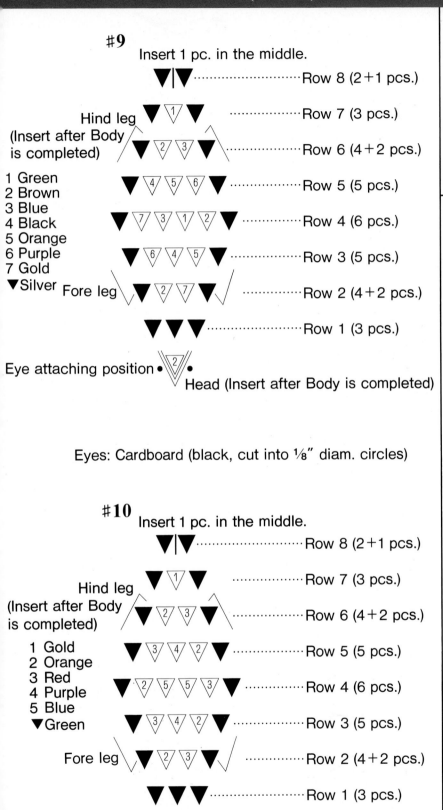

#9

Insert 1 pc. in the middle.

▼ | ▼ .... Row 8 (2+1 pcs.)

Hind leg ▼ ① ▼ .... Row 7 (3 pcs.)
(Insert after Body
is completed) ▼ ② ③ ▼ .... Row 6 (4+2 pcs.)

1 Green   ▼ ④ ⑤ ⑥ ▼ .... Row 5 (5 pcs.)
2 Brown
3 Blue   ▼ ⑦ ③ ① ② ▼ .... Row 4 (6 pcs.)
4 Black
5 Orange   ▼ ⑥ ④ ⑤ ▼ .... Row 3 (5 pcs.)
6 Purple
7 Gold Fore leg ▼ ② ⑦ ▼ ...... Row 2 (4+2 pcs.)
▼ Silver

     ▼ ▼ ▼ .... Row 1 (3 pcs.)

Eye attaching position • ▽② ▽ •
        Head (Insert after Body is completed)

Eyes: Cardboard (black, cut into ⅛″ diam. circles)

#10

Insert 1 pc. in the middle.

▼ | ▼ .... Row 8 (2+1 pcs.)

Hind leg ▼ ① ▼ .... Row 7 (3 pcs.)
(Insert after Body
is completed) ▼ ② ③ ▼ .... Row 6 (4+2 pcs.)

1 Gold   ▼ ③ ④ ② ▼ .... Row 5 (5 pcs.)
2 Orange
3 Red   ▼ ② ⑤ ⑤ ③ ▼ .... Row 4 (6 pcs.)
4 Purple
5 Blue   ▼ ③ ④ ② ▼ .... Row 3 (5 pcs.)
▼ Green

   Fore leg ▼ ② ③ ▼ .... Row 2 (4+2 pcs.)

     ▼ ▼ ▼ .... Row 1 (3 pcs.)

Eye attaching position • ▽ ▼ ▽ •
        Head (Insert after Body is completed)

#9
Completed size
2¾″ wide, 2⅜″ long
Materials
24 1½″×3″ rectangles of origami paper (silver)
 4 1½″×3″ rectangles of origami paper (brown)
 2 1½″×3″ rectangles of origami paper
   (green, blue, black, purple, orange, gold)
2 ⅛″ diam. eyes (black cardboard)

#10
Completed size
2¾″ wide, 2⅜″ long
Materials
25 1¾″×3½″ rectangles of paper (green)
 5 1¾″×3½″ rectangles of paper (orange)
 5 1¾″×3½″ rectangles of paper (red)
 2 1¾″×3½″ rectangles of paper (blue)
 2 1¾″×3½″ rectangles of paper (purple)
 1 1¾″×3½″ rectangle of paper (gold)
2 ⅛″ diam. eyes (black cardboard)
∗ Patterned *washi* paper is used here.

#11—#15
Completed size
2⅜″ wide, 2⅜″ long
Materials
40 1½″×3″ rectangles of origami paper
   (blue for #11, red for #12, orange for #13,
   brown for #14, pale green for #15)
2 ⅛″ diam. plastic eyes each
∗ Gradated origami paper is used here.

←See P.8–9 for step-by-step instructions.

#52 & #53 RED CROWNED CRANE (P.21)

Completed size
#52: 6" wide, 12" high
#53: 5" wide, 10" high

Materials

#52: 365   3¼" × 4½" rectangles of 1-ply board (white)
       3   3¼" × 4½" rectangles of textured paper (black)
     31   2¾" × 4½" rectangles of 1-ply board (white)
       1   2¾" × 4½" rectangle of textured paper (black)
       1   2¾" × 4½" rectangle of textured paper (red)
       2   ⅛" diam. plastic eyes

#53: 309   2⅜" × 4¼" rectangles of 1-ply board (white
     56   2⅜" × 4¼" rectangles of 1-ply board (blue)
       3   2⅜" × 4¼" rectangles of textured paper (bla
     31   2" × 3½" rectangles of 1-ply board (white)
       1   2" × 3½" rectangle of textured paper (blac
       1   2" × 3½" rectangle of textured paper (red)
       2   ⅛" diam. plastic eyes

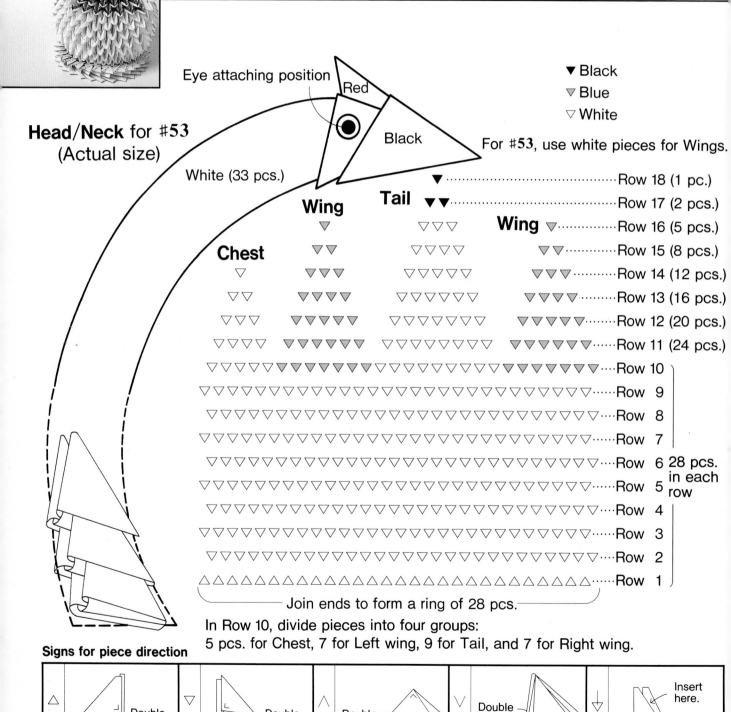

Eye attaching position

Red

▼ Black
▽ Blue
▽ White

Head/Neck for #53
(Actual size)

For #53, use white pieces for Wings.

White (33 pcs.)

Black

Wing   **Tail** ▼▼ ·································· Row 18 (1 pc.)
▽   ▼▼ ·································· Row 17 (2 pcs.)

Chest   ▽   ▽▽▽   **Wing** ▽ ·············· Row 16 (5 pcs.)
▽▽   ▽▽▽▽   ▽▽ ·········· Row 15 (8 pcs.)
▽   ▽▽▽   ▽▽▽▽▽   ▽▽▽ ········· Row 14 (12 pcs.)
▽▽   ▽▽▽▽   ▽▽▽▽▽▽   ▽▽▽▽ ········ Row 13 (16 pcs.)
▽▽▽   ▽▽▽▽▽   ▽▽▽▽▽▽▽   ▽▽▽▽▽ ····· Row 12 (20 pcs.)
▽▽▽▽   ▽▽▽▽▽▽   ▽▽▽▽▽▽▽▽   ▽▽▽▽▽▽ ···· Row 11 (24 pcs.)

Row 10
Row 9
Row 8
Row 7
Row 6   28 pcs. in each row
Row 5
Row 4
Row 3
Row 2
Row 1

Join ends to form a ring of 28 pcs.

In Row 10, divide pieces into four groups:
5 pcs. for Chest, 7 for Left wing, 9 for Tail, and 7 for Right wing.

Signs for piece direction

| △ | Double pocket | ▽ | Double pocket | ∧ | Double pocket | ∨ | Double pocket | ↓ | Insert here. |

#54 PEDESTAL (P.21)

Completed size
7" diameter

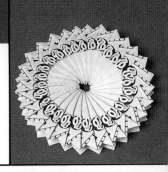

Materials
For #52: 32 3½" × 5" rectangles of 1-ply board
For #53: 28 3½" × 5" rectangles of 1-ply board

Note
The completed project may look different depending on the thickness of the paper used.

How to fold pieces

Head/Neck for #52
(Actual size)

Red

Black

Eye attaching position

White (31 pcs.)

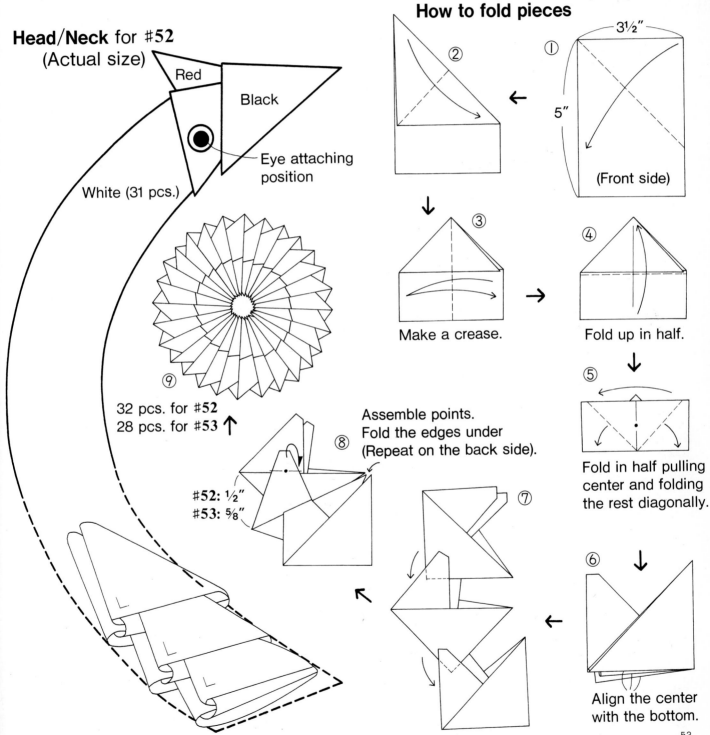

① 3½" 5" (Front side)

②

③ Make a crease.

④ Fold up in half.

⑤ Fold in half pulling center and folding the rest diagonally.

⑥ Align the center with the bottom.

⑦

⑧ Assemble points.
Fold the edges under
(Repeat on the back side).

#52: ½"
#53: ⅝"

⑨
32 pcs. for #52
28 pcs. for #53 ↑

53

Materials
#44: 285 1½"×3" rectangles of craft paper (black)
    52 1½"×3" rectangles of craft paper (white)
     1 1½"×3" rectangle of craft paper (red)
#45: 286 1½"×3" rectangles of craft paper (red)
    52 1½"×3" rectangles of craft paper (white)

16" ¼" ribbon
 1 ½" diam. sequins
 1 pearl-headed marking pin
＊Materials except rectangular paper counts
each item.
Note
The completed project may look diffe
depending on the thickness of the paper used

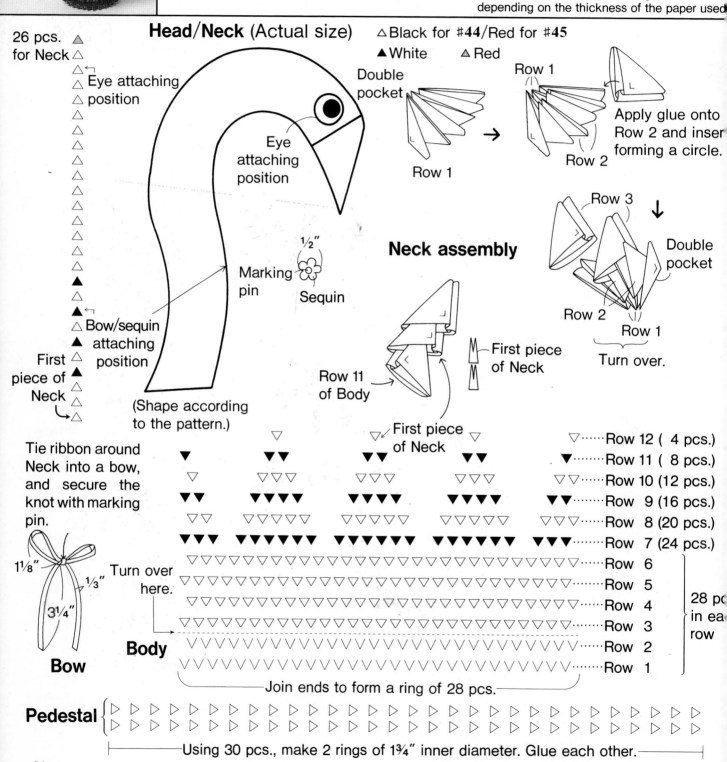

Head/Neck (Actual size)

26 pcs. △
for Neck △

△ Black for #44/Red for #45
▲ White   △ Red

Double pocket

Row 1

Row 1
Row 2

Apply glue onto Row 2 and inser forming a circle.

Eye attaching position

Eye attaching position

Row 3

Row 2

Row 1

Double pocket

Turn over.

Neck assembly

Row 11 of Body

First piece of Neck

First piece of Neck

Marking pin

½"

Sequin

Bow/sequin attaching position

First piece of Neck

(Shape according to the pattern.)

Tie ribbon around Neck into a bow, and secure the knot with marking pin.

▽······ Row 12 (4 pcs.)
▼······ Row 11 (8 pcs.)
▽▽····· Row 10 (12 pcs.)
▼▼····· Row 9 (16 pcs.)
▽▽▽···· Row 8 (20 pcs.)
▼▼▼····· Row 7 (24 pcs.)
Row 6
Row 5
Row 4
Row 3
Row 2
Row 1

28 pc
in ea
row

1⅛"
⅓"
3¼"

Turn over here.

Body

Join ends to form a ring of 28 pcs.

Bow

Pedestal

Using 30 pcs., make 2 rings of 1¾" inner diameter. Glue each other.

❶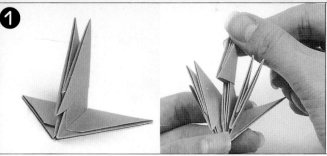

Row 1: Put a pair, double pockets down. Apply glue onto center 2 points and insert them into a piece held in the same direction. Make 14 of this 3-pc set. Row 2: Join 2 sets with 1 piece held in the same direction. Continue to join all sets.

❷

Turn over and join into a ring with a piece.

❸

Turn over and work Row 3 as directed in the diagram on opposite page, interlocking at an angle so as to form a ball shape.

❹

Work Rows 4-6 in the same manner. All pieces are glued together.

❺

Divide into quarters, and join 6 pcs. to each, in a contrasting color.

❻

Rows 8-12: Decrease the number of pieces as directed, changing color as well.

❼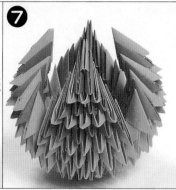

Onto 1 point, add 1 piece in opposite direction to make base of neck.

❽

Form neck interlocking 25 pcs. as directed.

❾

Tie ribbon around neck and make a bow. Attach a sequin by pushing marking pin into the knot.

❿

Make a pair of pedestals and glue them together.

⓫

Place SWAN on the pedestal and glue to secure.

Pieces used in the actual project are smaller.   55

Materials
519 1½"×3" rectangles of craft paper
(patterned gold-red for #46, pink for #47, white for #48)
1 1½"×3" rectangle of craft paper (red)
16" ¼" ribbon
1 ½" diam. sequin
1 pearl-headed marking pin
✳Materials except rectangular paper count for each item.

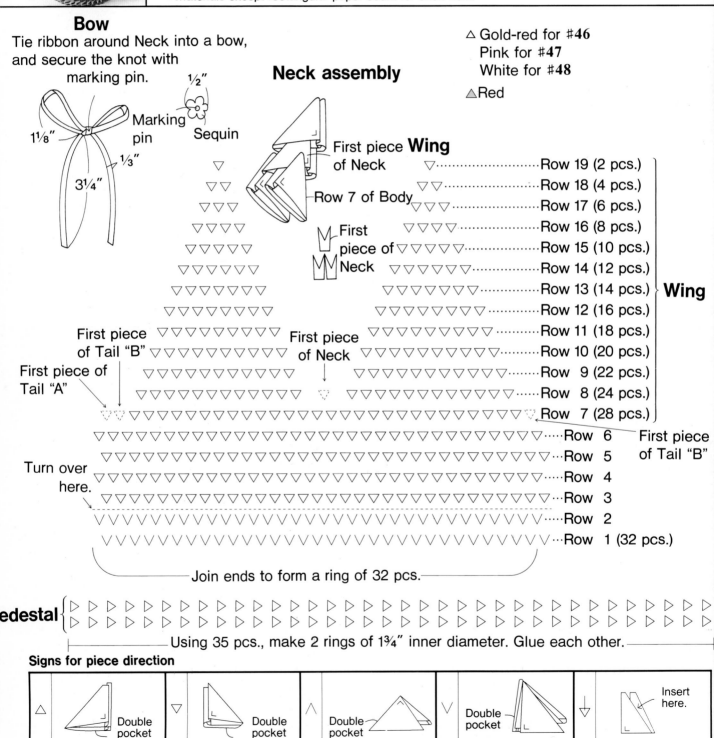

Bow
Tie ribbon around Neck into a bow, and secure the knot with marking pin.

△ Gold-red for #46
Pink for #47
White for #48

▲Red

Neck assembly

First piece of Neck **Wing**

Row 7 of Body

First piece of Neck

▽ .... Row 19 (2 pcs.)
.... Row 18 (4 pcs.)
.... Row 17 (6 pcs.)
.... Row 16 (8 pcs.)
.... Row 15 (10 pcs.)
.... Row 14 (12 pcs.)
.... Row 13 (14 pcs.)
.... Row 12 (16 pcs.)
.... Row 11 (18 pcs.)
.... Row 10 (20 pcs.)
.... Row 9 (22 pcs.)
.... Row 8 (24 pcs.)
.... Row 7 (28 pcs.)

Wing

First piece of Tail "A"
First piece of Tail "B"

First piece of Tail "B"

...........Row 6
...........Row 5

Turn over here.

...........Row 4
...........Row 3
...........Row 2
...........Row 1 (32 pcs.)

Join ends to form a ring of 32 pcs.

Pedestal
Using 35 pcs., make 2 rings of 1¾" inner diameter. Glue each other.

Signs for piece direction

△ Double pocket	▽ Double pocket	∧ Double pocket	∨ Double pocket	↓ Insert here.

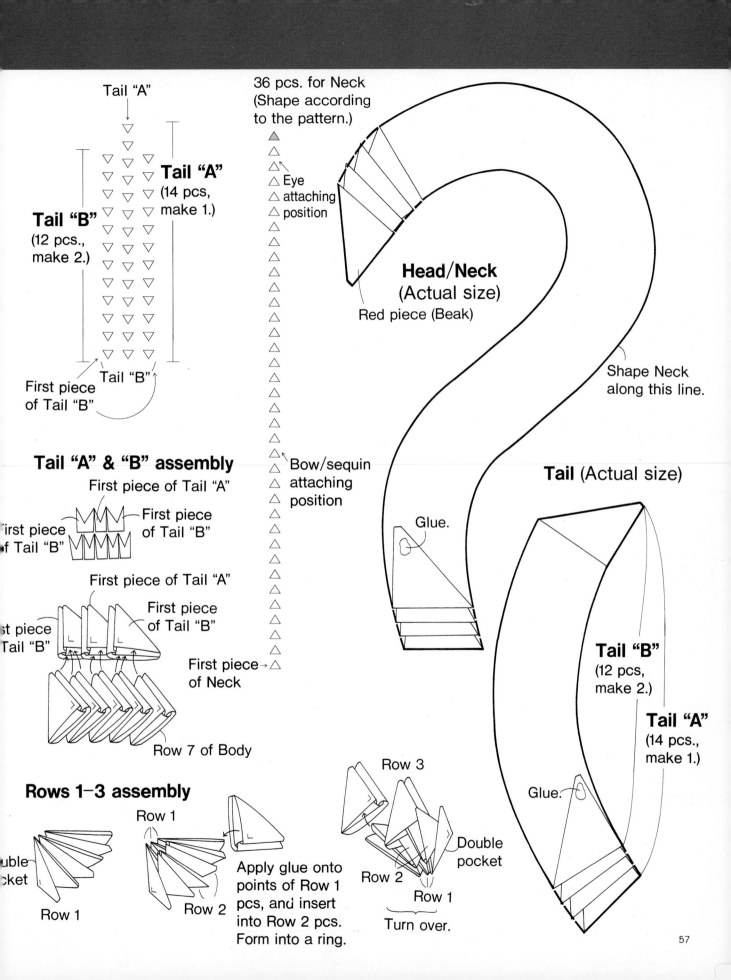

Tail "A"

Tail "A"
(14 pcs,
make 1.)

Tail "B"
(12 pcs.,
make 2.)

First piece
of Tail "B"

Tail "B"

36 pcs. for Neck
(Shape according
to the pattern.)

Eye
attaching
position

Bow/sequin
attaching
position

First piece
of Neck

Tail "A" & "B" assembly

First piece of Tail "A"

First piece
of Tail "B"

First piece
of Tail "B"

First piece of Tail "A"

First piece
of Tail "B"

First piece
of Tail "B"

Row 7 of Body

Rows 1-3 assembly

Double
pocket

Row 1

Row 1

Row 1

Row 2

Apply glue onto
points of Row 1
pcs, and insert
into Row 2 pcs.
Form into a ring.

Row 3

Row 2

Row 1

Double
pocket

Turn over.

Head/Neck
(Actual size)

Red piece (Beak)

Shape Neck
along this line.

Glue.

Tail (Actual size)

Tail "B"
(12 pcs,
make 2.)

Tail "A"
(14 pcs.,
make 1.)

Glue.

1

Put 2 pcs. double folds down. Join them by inserting the adjoining points into 1 pc. held in the same direction.

2

Make 16 sets. Join them in the same manner as Step 1, and form into a ring with 32 pcs.

3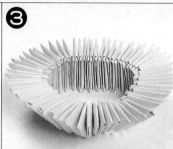

Turn over so Row 1 faces up.

4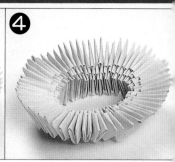

Work on Row 3 as directed in the diagram on previous page.

5

When Row 6 is done, divide pieces into three: Right wing (14), neck(1), left wing(14) and tail(3).

6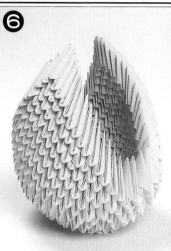

Form wings as directed in the diagram, forming a curvy outline.

7

Make neck and head as directed and interlock with body.

8

Make three tails as directed, according to the actual size pattern.

9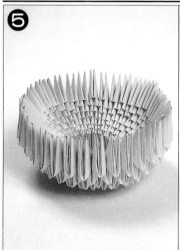

Attach tails as shown.

10

Tie ribbon around neck. Attach a sequin by pushing a marking pin into the knot. Attach eyes.

11

Make two pedestals and glue together.

12

Place SWAN on the pedestal and glue to secure.

❶

Place a pair of pieces double pockets down.

❷

Join them with a piece held in the same direction. Make another 3-pc set and join with a piece as shown.

❸

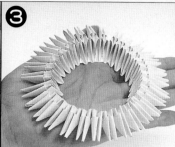

Make 15 sets in all and form a ring. Turn over.

❹

Applying glue, work Row 3 to Row 8 as directed in the diagram overleaf, changing colors as well.

❺

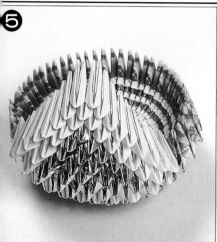

Row 9: Make chest. Join 6 patterned pcs. and add 2 solid (white) pcs. onto each side. Work as directed.

❻

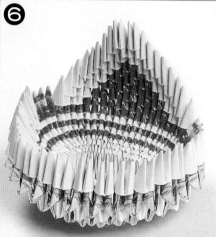

Row 9: Make tail feathers. Join 16 pcs., leaving 2 pcs.. of previous row unworked, on each side.

❼

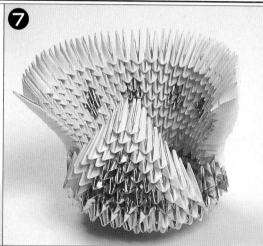

Rows 10-32: Construct fanned feathers by increasing 1 pc. on every row, altering colors as directed.

❽

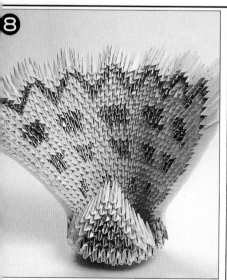

Rows 33-39: Decrease 1 pc. in every row as directed. Tail feather is completed.

❾

Make neck and head. Glue on crest and eyes. Push in marking pins to finish.

❿

Make pedestal in the same manner as Rows 1 to 3.

⓫

Place PEACOCK on the pedestal and glue to secure.

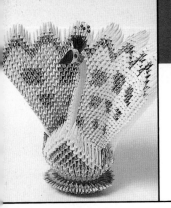

#49 & #50 PEACOCK (P.20)

Completed size
#49: 8" wide, 5" high
#50: 10" wide, 9" high

Materials
#49: 954 ¾" × 1¾" rectangles of craft paper (white)
313 ¾" × 1¾" rectangles of craft paper (patterned red)
3 ¾" × 1¾" rectangles of craft paper (red for beak and crest)
2 ⅛" diam. plastic eyes
5 pearl-headed marking pins (assorted colors)

#50: 954 1¼" × 2⅜" rectangles of craft paper (cream)
317 1¼" × 2⅜" rectangles of craft paper (patterned red)
3 1¼" × 2⅜" rectangles of craft paper (red for beak and crest)
2 ¼" diam. plastic eyes
6 pearl-headed marking (assorted colors)

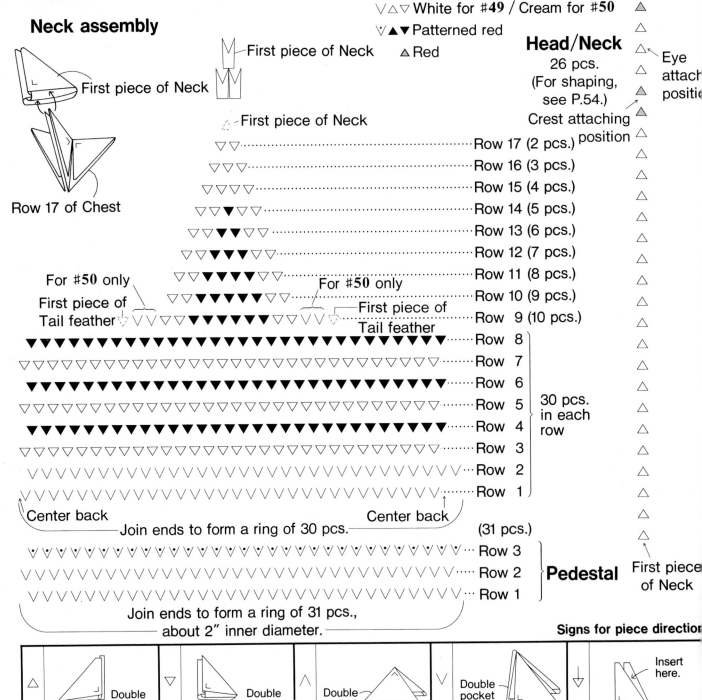

Neck assembly

∨△▽ White for #49 / Cream for #50
∨▲▼ Patterned red
△ Red

First piece of Neck
First piece of Neck
First piece of Neck

Head/Neck
26 pcs.
(For shaping, see P.54.)
Crest attaching position
Eye attach position

Row 17 of Chest

For #50 only
First piece of Tail feather

For #50 only
First piece of Tail feather

Row 17 (2 pcs.)
Row 16 (3 pcs.)
Row 15 (4 pcs.)
Row 14 (5 pcs.)
Row 13 (6 pcs.)
Row 12 (7 pcs.)
Row 11 (8 pcs.)
Row 10 (9 pcs.)
Row 9 (10 pcs.)
Row 8
Row 7
Row 6
Row 5
Row 4
Row 3
Row 2
Row 1

30 pcs. in each row

Center back
Center back
(31 pcs.)
Join ends to form a ring of 30 pcs.

Row 3
Row 2
Row 1

Pedestal
First piece of Neck

Join ends to form a ring of 31 pcs., about 2" inner diameter.

Signs for piece direction

△ Double pocket	▽ Double pocket	∧ Double pocket	∨ Double pocket	↓ Insert here.

Tail feathers

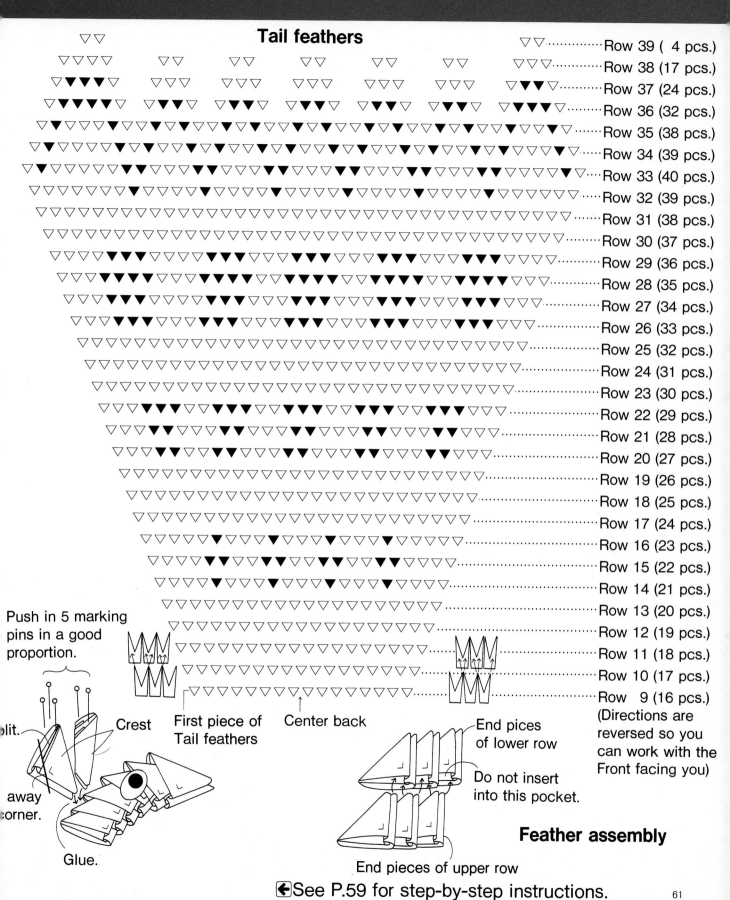

Row 39 (4 pcs.)
Row 38 (17 pcs.)
Row 37 (24 pcs.)
Row 36 (32 pcs.)
Row 35 (38 pcs.)
Row 34 (39 pcs.)
Row 33 (40 pcs.)
Row 32 (39 pcs.)
Row 31 (38 pcs.)
Row 30 (37 pcs.)
Row 29 (36 pcs.)
Row 28 (35 pcs.)
Row 27 (34 pcs.)
Row 26 (33 pcs.)
Row 25 (32 pcs.)
Row 24 (31 pcs.)
Row 23 (30 pcs.)
Row 22 (29 pcs.)
Row 21 (28 pcs.)
Row 20 (27 pcs.)
Row 19 (26 pcs.)
Row 18 (25 pcs.)
Row 17 (24 pcs.)
Row 16 (23 pcs.)
Row 15 (22 pcs.)
Row 14 (21 pcs.)
Row 13 (20 pcs.)
Row 12 (19 pcs.)
Row 11 (18 pcs.)
Row 10 (17 pcs.)
Row 9 (16 pcs.)
(Directions are reversed so you can work with the Front facing you)

Push in 5 marking pins in a good proportion.

Split.

Crest

First piece of Tail feathers

Center back

away corner.

Glue.

End pices of lower row

Do not insert into this pocket.

Feather assembly

End pieces of upper row

⬅See P.59 for step-by-step instructions.

61

#51 DANCING CRANE (P.20)

Completed size
5½″ wide, 13″ high

Materials
288 1½″ × 2¾″ rectangles of craft paper (white)
 35 1⅛″ × 2¼″ rectangles of craft paper (black)
 32 1⅛″ × 2¼″ rectangles of craft paper (white)
  7 2¼″ × 4″ rectangles of craft paper (black)
  1 1½″ × 1½″ rectangle of craft paper (yellow)
  1 1⅛″ × 2¼″ rectangle of craft paper (red)

2 ⅛″ diam. plastic eyes
20″ ⅛″ diam. cord
4 ft. 1/16″ diam. wire
26″ 1/20″ diam. wire
7 ft. ½″ floral tape
2 B3 boards
Tissue paper

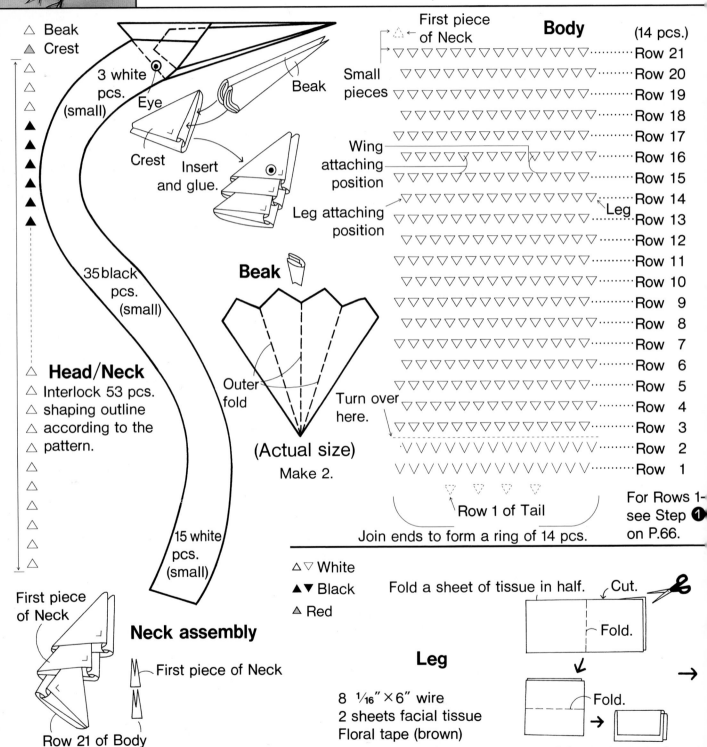

△ Beak
▲ Crest

3 white
pcs.
(small)

Eye

Beak

Crest   Insert
and glue.

35 black
pcs.
(small)

Head/Neck
△ Interlock 53 pcs.
△ shaping outline
△ according to the
△ pattern.

Beak

Outer
fold

(Actual size)
Make 2.

15 white
pcs.
(small)

First piece
of Neck

Neck assembly

First piece of Neck

Row 21 of Body

First piece
of Neck   **Body**   (14 pcs.)

Small
pieces

Wing
attaching
position

Leg attaching
position

Turn over
here.

Row 21
Row 20
Row 19
Row 18
Row 17
Row 16
Row 15
Row 14   Leg
Row 13
Row 12
Row 11
Row 10
Row 9
Row 8
Row 7
Row 6
Row 5
Row 4
Row 3
Row 2
Row 1

Row 1 of Tail

Join ends to form a ring of 14 pcs.

For Rows 1–
see Step ❶
on P.66.

△▽ White
▲▼ Black
△ Red

Fold a sheet of tissue in half.   Cut.

Fold.

Leg
8 1/16″ × 6″ wire
2 sheets facial tissue
Floral tape (brown)

Fold.

Slide 1 sheet to form
a smooth edge.

1. **Make 2 copies of Wing ③** (Overleaf).

Board — Glue.
Copy of Wing ③

2. **Cut out Wings, 2 pairs in all.**

Copy of Wing ③
Cut out.

3. **Layer front and back side of Wing, and glue.**

Wing ③

4. **Make slits into Wing ③.**
Slit only into lower feathers.
Do not slit top layer.
Wing ③

5. **Make 2 copies of Wing ① and ②.**

Board — Glue onto board.
Copy of Wing ②
Cut out and make a pair.

Copy of Wing ①
Apply glue on back side.
Cut out and make a pair.

6. **Make slits into Wings ① and ②.**

Wing ①
Do not slit top layer.
Slit only into lower feathers.

Wing ②
Do not slit top layer.
Slit only into lower feathers.

7. **Glue Wing ① and Wing ②, front sides up.**

Wing ①   Glue.
Wing ①
Wing ②
Wing ②

8. **Shape wire to align with upper curve of Wing ③.**

Bend 13" wire into half.
Thread wire through cord and shape.
Wire
Fix wire and cord with ample amount of glue.
Glue ¹⁄₁₂" inside of paper.
Let 1" of wire out.
Wing ③

9. **Glue Wings made in Step 7 (above) onto Wing ③.**

Glue on.
Wing ①
Wing ②
Wing ③

---

2 pcs. | Bind 4 pcs. of wire.
6"
1 pc.
1 pc.
Bend into a right angle.
1½"
1¼"
¾"
Tape. →
Pull tape as you work.

Secure with adhesive tape.
Wrap with floral tape:
Tape around the bend 2-3 times tightly, then wrap up for 3½".

Glue.
Wrap with tissue.

1"   Tape to cover tissue.
Make 2 legs.
Start taping here.
Form a lump with tape.
Leave ¹⁄₁₂"-⅛" of wire unwrapped.

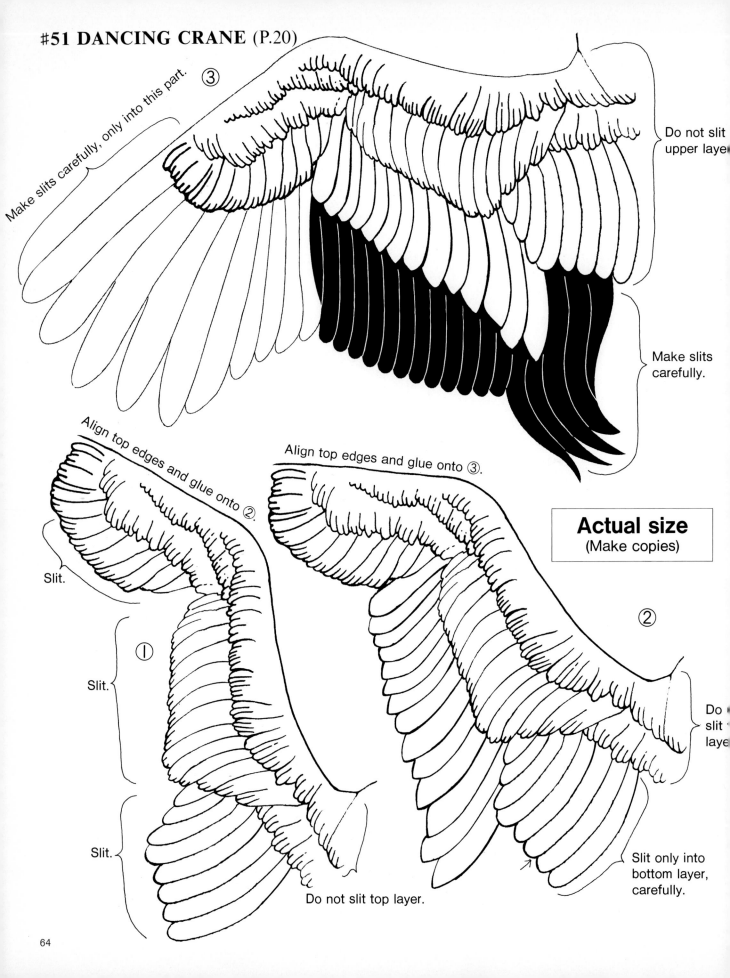

Make slits carefully, only into this part. ③

Do not slit upper layer

Make slits carefully.

Align top edges and glue onto ②.

Align top edges and glue onto ③.

Actual size
(Make copies)

Slit.

①

Slit.

②

Slit.

Do slit layer

Slit.

Do not slit top layer.

Slit only into bottom layer, carefully.

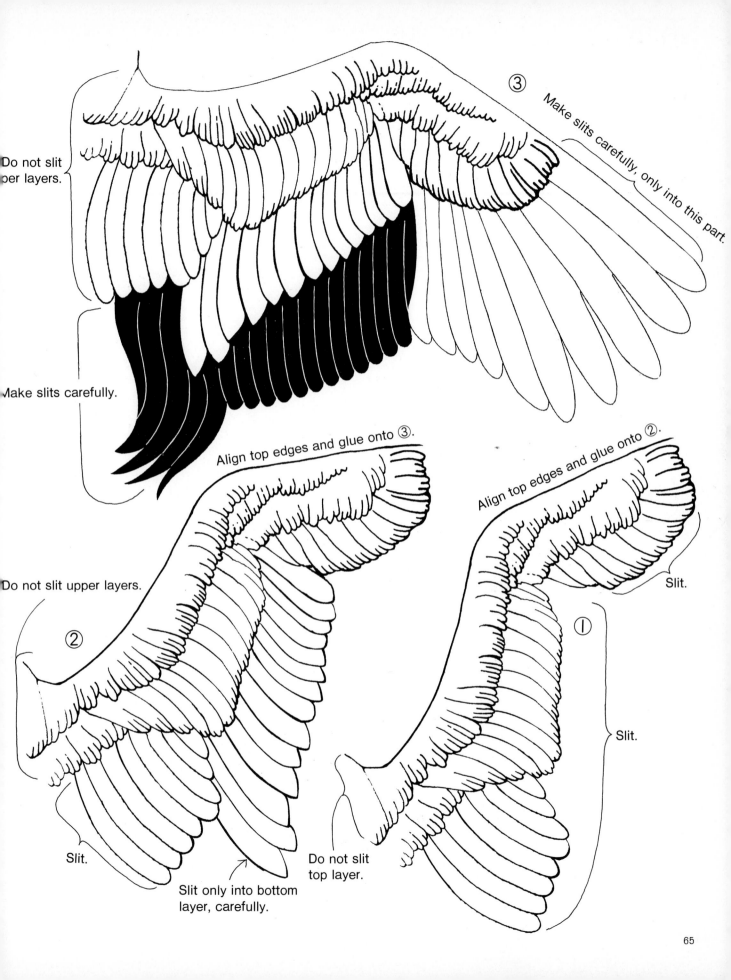

Do not slit
per layers.

③ Make slits carefully, only into this part.

Make slits carefully.

Align top edges and glue onto ③.

Align top edges and glue onto ②.

Do not slit upper layers.

②

①

Slit.

Slit.

Slit.

Do not slit
top layer.

Slit only into bottom
layer, carefully.

① Put a pair of pieces double pockets down. Join them with a piece held in the same direction. Make 7 sets. (14 pcs. on Rows 1 and 2)

② Join into a ring, by covering end pieces with a new piece.

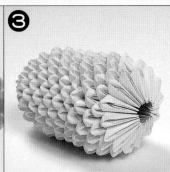

③ Rows 3-20: Applying glue each time, interlock 14 pcs. in each row, shaping the body.

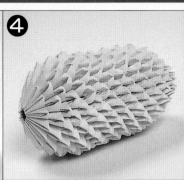

④ Row:21: Join 14 small pcs. without glue.

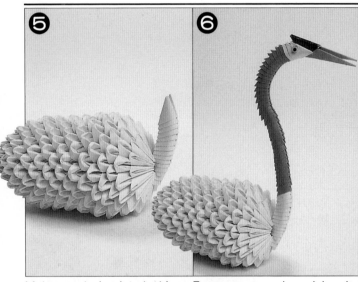

⑤ Make neck by interlocking 15 pcs. with glue. Attach to body so as to conceal the hole.

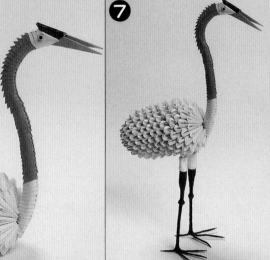

⑥ Form upper neck and head referring to diagram on P.62. Attach crest, eyes and beak.

⑦ Make legs as directed on P.63, and insert into the indicated positions with glue.

⑧ Make tail and glue onto at the indicated position.

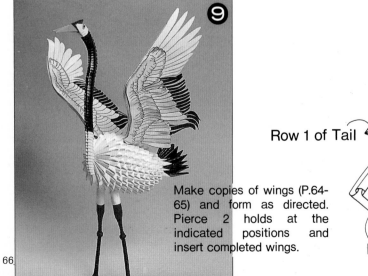

⑨ Make copies of wings (P.64-65) and form as directed. Pierce 2 holds at the indicated positions and insert completed wings.

Tail assembly

Apply glue between pieces.

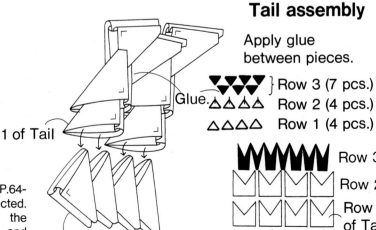

Glue. ▼▼▼ } Row 3 (7 pcs.)
△△△△ Row 2 (4 pcs.)
△△△△ Row 1 (4 pcs.)

Row 1 of Tail

Row 1 of Body

Row 3
Row 2
Row 1 of Tail
Row 1 of Body

#39 LEMON (P.17)

Completed size
2¼" wide, 1¾" high

Materials
30 1½"×3" rectangles of origami paper (yellow)
6 1½"×3" rectangles of origami paper (white)

Note
The completed project may look different depending on the thickness of the paper used.

▽ Yellow   ▼ White

▽▽▽▽▽▽▽▽▽▽▽▽▽▽▽▽·······Row 6
▽▽▽▽▽▽▽▽▽▽▽▽▽▽▽▽·······Row 5
▽▽▽▽▽▽▽▽▽▽▽▽▽▽▽▽·······Row 4
▽▽▽▽▽▽▽▽▽▽▽▽▽▽▽▽·······Row 3
▼▼▼▼▼▼▼▼▼▼▼▼▼▼▼▼·······Row 2
△△△△△△△△△△△△△△△△·······Row 1

16 pcs. in each row.

Join ends to form
a ring of 16 pcs.

＊Pieces used in the actual project are smaller.

❶ Apply a dab of glue on single points of 3-4 yellow pcs., and paste them together.

❷ Continue until 16 pcs. are pasted. Join into a circle and put on double pockets.

❸ Row 2: Insert adjoining points into double pocket of a white piece. Continue.

❹ Row 3: Repeat with yellow pieces.

❺ Rows 4-6: Continue joining the same number of pieces, interlocking at an angle to shape. Glue top to secure.

❻ Turn over for completed LEMON.

#58

#57

Materials
#57: 52 each 1½"×3" rectangles of origami paper (4 colors)
     26 1½"×3" rectangles of origami paper (1 color)
     13 1½"×3" rectangles of origami paper (1 color)
     8" ½" ribbon
#58: 60 each 2"×3" rectangles of origami paper (10 colors)
     12" 1" ribbon
     1 miniature bell

Note
The completed project may look different depending on the thickness of the paper used.

❶

Apply a dab of glue on single points of 4-5 pcs., and paste them together. Make several sets.

❷
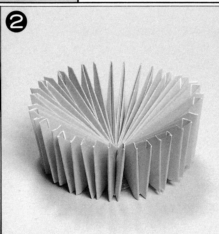

When 19(30 for #58) pcs. are used, paste each other and join into a circle.

❸
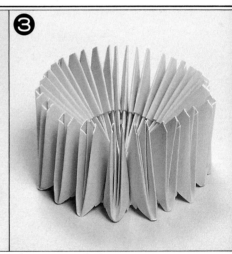

Row 2: Insert adjoining points of Row 1 into the double pocket of a piece. Continue all around.

❹
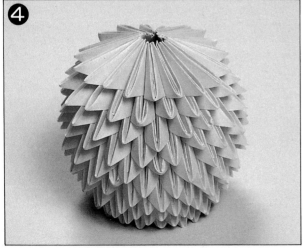

Row 3-18: Continue, altering colors as directed on the left page, and shaping into a ball with as small opening as possible.

❺
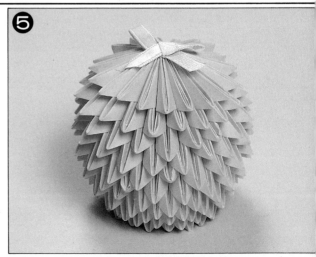

Cover the top with a bow. (Sew a miniature bell onto wrong side of the bow before attaching.)

#57

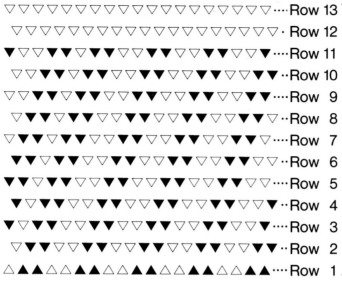

····Row 13
· Row 12
····Row 11
··Row 10
····Row 9
··Row 8
····Row 7
··Row 6
····Row 5
··Row 4
····Row 3
··Row 2
····Row 1

19 pcs. in each row.

Color is alternated every 2 pcs.

⎯ Join ends to form a ring of 19 pcs. ⎯

Make your favorite stripes
by arranging the color chart.

A repeated pattern consists of 10 colors.

#58

B C D E F G H I J A B C D E F G H I J A B C D E F G H I J A

··· Row 20
·Row 19
···Row 18
···Row 17
···Row 16
·Row 15
···Row 14
···Row 13
···Row 12
···Row 11
···Row 10
···Row 9
···Row 8
·Row 7
···Row 6
···Row 5
···Row 4
·Row 3
···Row 2
·Row 1

30 pcs. in each row.

⎯⎯⎯ Join ends to form a ring of 30 pcs. ⎯⎯⎯

#59–#61 GOOD-LUCK *HYOTAN* (GOURD) (P.23

Completed size
#59: 5½" wide, 10" high   #60: 5¼" wide, 9" high   #61: 4¼"wide, 7" high
Materials
#59: 762 2⅜" × 4¾" rectangles of *washi* paper (silver)
     3 ft. cord with fringe
#60: 762 3" × 6" rectangles of origami paper (pale green)
     ½ ft. cord with fringe
#61: 762 1¾" × 3¾" glossy paper (from magazine)
     ½ ft. cord with fringe

Row 19 & 20: Work in opposite direction.

▽▽▽▽▽▽▽▽▽▽▽▽▽▽▽▽▽▽▽▽·············Row 28
▽▽▽▽▽▽▽▽▽▽▽▽▽▽▽▽▽▽▽▽·············Row 27
▽▽▽▽▽▽▽▽▽▽▽▽▽▽▽▽▽▽▽▽·············Row 26
▽▽▽▽▽▽▽▽▽▽▽▽▽▽▽▽▽▽▽▽·············Row 25
▽▽▽▽▽▽▽▽▽▽▽▽▽▽▽▽▽▽▽▽·············Row 24
▽▽▽▽▽▽▽▽▽▽▽▽▽▽▽▽▽▽▽▽·············Row 23
▽▽▽▽▽▽▽▽▽▽▽▽▽▽▽▽▽▽▽▽·············Row 22
▽▽ ▽▽ ▽▽ ▽▽ ▽▽ ▽▽ ▽▽ ▽▽ ▽▽ ▽▽···Row 21
△△△△△△△△△△△△△△△△△△△△△△△△△△△△△△·····Row 20
△△△△△△△△△△△△△△△△△△△△△△△△△△△△△△···Row 19
▽▽▽▽▽▽▽▽▽▽▽▽▽▽▽▽▽▽▽▽▽▽▽▽▽▽▽▽▽▽▽▽·····Row 18
▽▽▽▽▽▽▽▽▽▽▽▽▽▽▽▽▽▽▽▽▽▽▽▽▽▽▽▽▽▽▽▽···Row 17
▽▽▽▽▽▽▽▽▽▽▽▽▽▽▽▽▽▽▽▽▽▽▽▽▽▽▽▽▽▽▽▽·····Row 16
▽▽▽▽▽▽▽▽▽▽▽▽▽▽▽▽▽▽▽▽▽▽▽▽▽▽▽▽▽▽▽▽···Row 15
▽▽▽▽▽▽▽▽▽▽▽▽▽▽▽▽▽▽▽▽▽▽▽▽▽▽▽▽▽▽▽▽···Row 14
▽▽▽▽▽▽▽▽▽▽▽▽▽▽▽▽▽▽▽▽▽▽▽▽▽▽▽▽▽▽▽▽···Row 13
▽▽▽▽▽▽▽▽▽▽▽▽▽▽▽▽▽▽▽▽▽▽▽▽▽▽▽▽▽▽▽▽·····Row 12
▽▽▽▽▽▽▽▽▽▽▽▽▽▽▽▽▽▽▽▽▽▽▽▽▽▽▽▽▽▽▽▽···Row 11
▽▽▽▽▽▽▽▽▽▽▽▽▽▽▽▽▽▽▽▽▽▽▽▽▽▽▽▽▽▽▽▽···Row 10
▽▽▽▽▽▽▽▽▽▽▽▽▽▽▽▽▽▽▽▽▽▽▽▽▽▽▽▽▽▽▽▽···Row 9
▽▽▽▽▽▽▽▽▽▽▽▽▽▽▽▽▽▽▽▽▽▽▽▽▽▽▽▽▽▽▽▽·····Row 8
▽▽▽▽▽▽▽▽▽▽▽▽▽▽▽▽▽▽▽▽▽▽▽▽▽▽▽▽▽▽▽▽···Row 7
▽▽▽▽▽▽▽▽▽▽▽▽▽▽▽▽▽▽▽▽▽▽▽▽▽▽▽▽▽▽▽▽·····Row 6
▽▽▽▽▽▽▽▽▽▽▽▽▽▽▽▽▽▽▽▽▽▽▽▽▽▽▽▽▽▽▽▽···Row 5
▽▽▽▽▽▽▽▽▽▽▽▽▽▽▽▽▽▽▽▽▽▽▽▽▽▽▽▽▽▽▽▽·····Row 4
▽▽▽▽▽▽▽▽▽▽▽▽▽▽▽▽▽▽▽▽▽▽▽▽▽▽▽▽▽▽▽▽···Row 3
▽▽▽▽▽▽▽▽▽▽▽▽▽▽▽▽▽▽▽▽▽▽▽▽▽▽▽▽▽▽▽▽·····Row 2
△△△△△△△△△△△△△△△△△△△△△△△△△△△△△△···Row 1

— Join ends to form a ring of 30 pcs. —

20 pcs. in each row

30 pcs. in each row

How to make stem

Cut rectangular paper in

Layer 4 sheets.

↓

Roll up and glue.

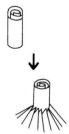

↓

Insert into center and glu

How to reduce in Row 21

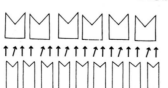

Row 21

Row 20

Repeat this to decrease the number
of pcs., from 30 to 20.

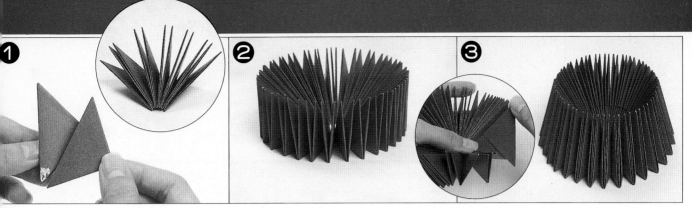

①
pply a dab of glue on single points of 5-6
cs., and paste them together. Repeat to
ake this set until 30 pcs. are used.

②
Paste each other and join into a circle of 30 pcs. (Row 1).

③
Row 2: Insert adjoining points of Row 1 into double pocket of a piece, double points facing up. Continue all around.

④
ows 3-18: Work in the same manner inter-
cking at an angle so as to form a ball.

⑤
Row 19: Change the direction of pieces.

⑥
Row 20: Work as for Row 18. Row 20: Change the direction of pieces again.

⑦
ow 21: Decrease the number of pieces
20. Insert 3 points into a double
cket so that 2 pcs. cover 3 pcs.

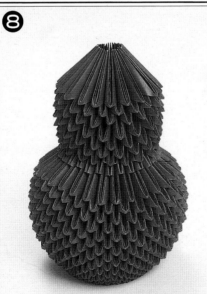

⑧
Rows 22-28: Work with 20 pcs. on every row.

⑨
Layer 4 rectangles and roll up to form stem. Glue onto top of gourd, and tie cord around the stem, into a bow.

#65–#67 WINGED OWL (P.24)

Completed size
7" wide, 6¾" high

Materials   <#65>   [#66] |#67|
317 2⅜" × 4¼" rectangles of craft paper <black> [brown] |moss green|
 81 2⅜" × 4¼" rectangles of craft paper <white> [white] |white|
  2 2⅜" × 4¼" rectangles of craft paper <dark brown> [dark brown] |dark brown|
  1 2⅜" × 4¼" rectangle of craft paper <pinl> [pink] |pink|
1 pearl-headed marking pin   <blue> [white] |yellow|
⅜" wide ribbon   <3" moss green> [8" green] |3" green|
2 ½" diam. plastic eyes each
1 ½" diam. bead wheel each

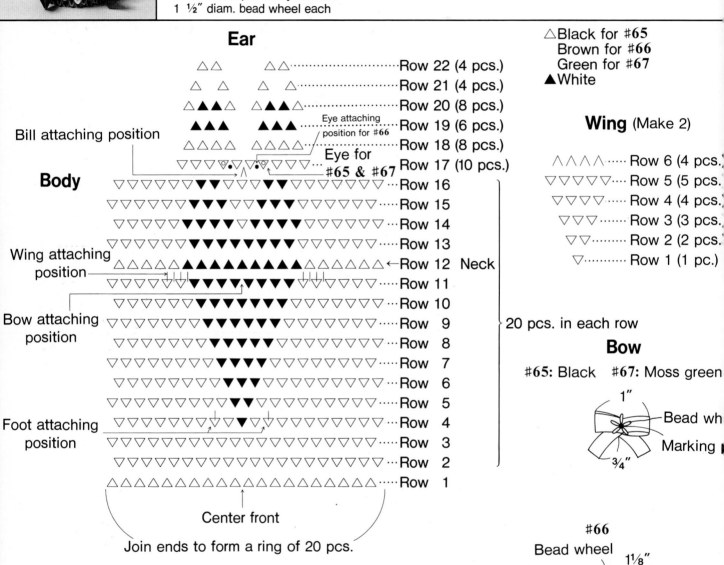

Ear

△Black for #65
Brown for #66
Green for #67
▲White

············· Row 22 (4 pcs.)
············· Row 21 (4 pcs.)
············· Row 20 (8 pcs.)
Eye attaching
position for #66 ···· Row 19 (6 pcs.)
············· Row 18 (8 pcs.)
Eye for
#65 & #67 ·· Row 17 (10 pcs.)

Body
Bill attaching position

Wing (Make 2)

∧∧∧∧ ····· Row 6 (4 pcs.)
▽▽▽▽▽ ···· Row 5 (5 pcs.)
▽▽▽▽ ····· Row 4 (4 pcs.)
▽▽▽ ······· Row 3 (3 pcs.)
▽▽ ········· Row 2 (2 pcs.)
▽ ·········· Row 1 (1 pc.)

Row 16
Row 15
Row 14
Row 13
←Row 12   Neck
Row 11
Row 10
Row 9
Row 8
Row 7
Row 6
Row 5
Row 4
Row 3
Row 2
Row 1

Wing attaching position
Bow attaching position
Foot attaching position

} 20 pcs. in each row

Center front

Join ends to form a ring of 20 pcs.

Bow
#65: Black   #67: Moss green

1"
Bead wh
Marking
¾"

#66
Bead wheel
1⅛"
Marking pin
1¾"

Signs for piece direction

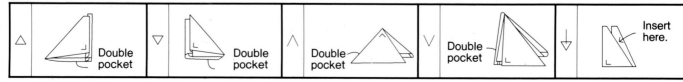

| △ | Double pocket | ▽ | Double pocket | ∧ | Double pocket | ∨ | Double pocket | ↓ | Insert here. |

72

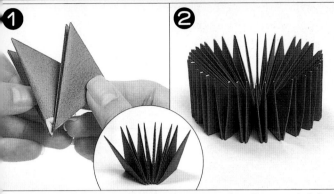

❶

Apply a dab of glue on single points of 5-6 pcs., and paste them together. Repeat to make this set until 20 pcs. are used.

❷

Paste each other and join into a circle of 20 pcs. (Row 1).

❸

Row 2: Insert adjoining points of Row 1 into double pocket of a piece, double points facing up. Continue all around.

❹

Rows 3-11: Continue joining the same number of pieces, altering color as directed on the opposite page.

❺

Row 12: Change the direction of pieces so the right angles face outward. See diagram for color layout.

❻

Rows 13-16: Change the direction of pieces again so the right angles face inward. See diagram for color layout.

❼

Row 17: Begin at center front; join 5 pcs. each rightward and leftward. Insert a pink piece into center front.

❽

Rows 18-22: Change the direction of pieces again and form ears, one by one.

❾

Both ears are completed.

❿

Make a wing referring to the diagram. Make 2.

⓫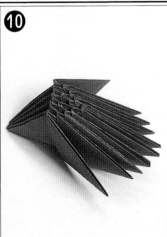

Insert wings into indicated positions.

⓬

Insert feet into indicated positions. Attach eyes and bow to finish.

#75 BRIDEGROOM (P.26)

Completed size
4¼" wide, 5½" high

Materials
274 2⅜" × 4¾" rectangles of craft paper (purple)
102 2⅜" × 4¾" rectangles of craft paper (gray)
 62 2⅜" × 4¾" rectangles of craft paper (white)
  1 2⅜" × 4¾" rectangle of craft paper (pink)
2 pearl-headed marking pins (purple & white)
12" ¼" ribbon (purple)   2 ½" diam. plastic eyes   1 ½" diam. bead wheel   2 silk flowers (pink)

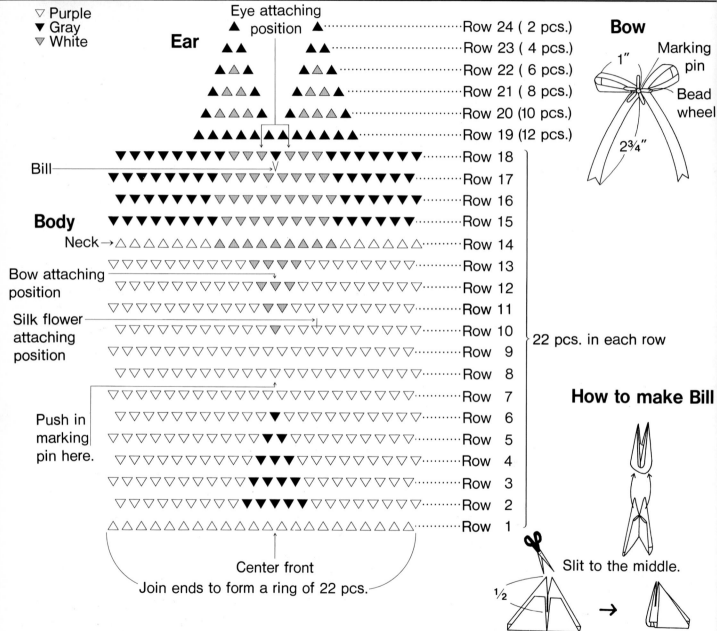

▽ Purple
▼ Gray
▽ White

Ear

Eye attaching
▲ position ▲ ···················· Row 24 (2 pcs.)
▲▲   ▲▲ ···················· Row 23 (4 pcs.)
▲▲▲   ▲▲▲ ···················· Row 22 (6 pcs.)
▲▲▲▲   ▲▲▲▲ ···················· Row 21 (8 pcs.)
▲▲▲▲▲   ▲▲▲▲▲ ···················· Row 20 (10 pcs.)
▲▲▲▲▲▲ ▲▲▲▲▲▲ ···················· Row 19 (12 pcs.)

Bill ─────→ ····················· Row 18
····················· Row 17
····················· Row 16

Body ····················· Row 15

Neck → ····················· Row 14

Bow attaching
position ····················· Row 13
····················· Row 12

Silk flower
attaching
position ····················· Row 11
····················· Row 10
····················· Row 9
····················· Row 8
····················· Row 7

Push in
marking
pin here. ····················· Row 6
····················· Row 5
····················· Row 4
····················· Row 3
····················· Row 2
····················· Row 1

Center front
Join ends to form a ring of 22 pcs.

22 pcs. in each row

Bow

Marking
pin
Bead
wheel
1"
2¾"

How to make Bill

Slit to the middle.
½

➡ See P.77 for step-by-step instructions.

Signs for piece direction

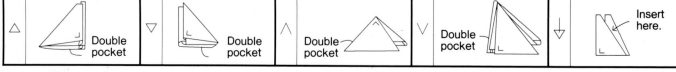

△ Double pocket	▽ Double pocket	∧ Double pocket	∨ Double pocket	⬇ Insert here.

74

Completed size
4¼" wide, 6" high

Materials
399 2⅜"×4¾" rectangles of craft paper (white)
 75 2⅜"×4¾" rectangles of craft paper (pink)
  1 2⅜"×4¾" rectangle of craft paper (gold)
  1 2⅜"×4¾" rectangle of craft paper (red)
2 ½" diam. plastic eyes
1 pearl-headed marking pin (white)

16" ¼" ribbon (silver)
115 ⅛" diam. perl beads
1 ½" diam. bead wheel
3 silk flowers (pink)
12"×13" dotted tulle

Sew on beads omitting the center of veil, in a flower pattern (See bottom).

Veil

1⅛"
2⅜"
2⅜" 4" 2⅜"
⅜"
½" ½" ¾" ¾"
Silk flower
¾"
Silk flower attaching position

Veil
12"
(6" for kid owl)
Center front
— 13" —
(6½" for kid owl)

△ White
▲ Pink
△ Gold

Ear

Silk flower attaching position

Eye attaching position

Bill

Bow attaching position

Center front

△ .... Row 23 (2 pcs.)
△△ .... Row 22 (4 pcs.)
△△△ .... Row 21 (6 pcs.)
△△△△ .... Row 20 (8 pcs.)
△△△△△ .... Row 19 (10 pcs.)
△△△▲▲▲△△△ .... Row 18 (12 pcs.)
▽▽▽▽▽▽▽▽▽▽ .... Row 17
▽▽▽▽▽▽▽▽▽▽ .... Row 16
▽▽▽▽▽▽▽▽▽▽ .... Row 15
△△△△△△△△△△ .... Row 14
△△△△▲△△△△△ ← Row 13 | Neck
▽▽▽▼▼▽▽▽▽ .... Row 12
▽▽▽▽▼▽▽▽▽ .... Row 11
▽▽▼▽▼▽▽▽ .... Row 10
▽▼▽▼▽▽▽ .... Row 9
▽▼▽▼▼▽▽ .... Row 8
▽▽▽▽▽▽▽ .... Row 7
▽▽▼▽▼▽▽ .... Row 6
▽▼▽▼▽▽ .... Row 5
▽▽▽▽▽▽ .... Row 4
▽▼▽▽▽▽ .... Row 3
▽▽▼▼▼▽▽ .... Row 2
▲▲▲▲▲▲▲▲▲▲▲▲ .... Row 1

22 pcs. in each row

Body

Center front
Join ends to form a ring of 22 pcs.

➡See P.77 for step-by-step instructions.

How to secure beads

①Using a threaded needle, sew on bead twice.

②Apply a dab of glue onto the first stitch.

③Tie into a knot winding twice, before the glue becomes dry.

④When the glue is dry, trim away excess thread.

Bead embroidery pattern

Perl bead — Dot of the tulle

Back side
Tulle →
(cross section)
Front side
Bead
Glue

#62–#64 OWL (P.24)

Completed size
4" wide, 6½" high

Materials

	⟨#62⟩	[#63]	⟨#64⟩
328 2"×3½" rectangles of craft paper	⟨yellow⟩	[blue]	⟨pink⟩
88 2"×3½" rectangles of craft paper	⟨white⟩	[white]	⟨white⟩
1 2"×3½" rectangle of craft paper	⟨red⟩	[red]	⟨red⟩
1 pearl-headed marking pin	⟨white⟩	[white]	⟨white⟩
8" ¼" ribbon	⟨yellow⟩	[blue]	⟨pink⟩
1 ½" diam. bead wheel	⟨white⟩	[blue]	⟨pink⟩
2 ½" diam. plastic eyes each			

△ Yellow for **#62**
Blue for **#63**
Pink for **#64**
▲ White

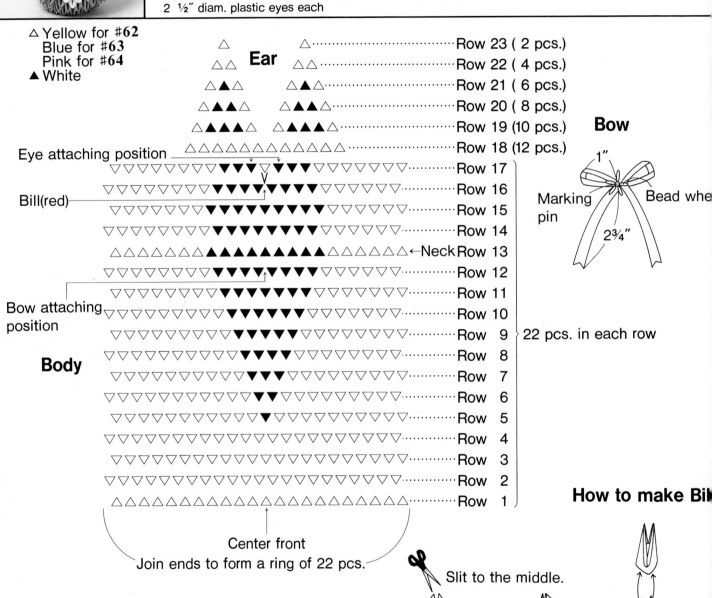

Ear

Row 23 (2 pcs.)
Row 22 (4 pcs.)
Row 21 (6 pcs.)
Row 20 (8 pcs.)
Row 19 (10 pcs.)
Row 18 (12 pcs.)

Eye attaching position —— Row 17
Row 16
Bill(red) —— Row 15
Row 14
←Neck Row 13
Row 12
Row 11
Bow attaching position —— Row 10
Row 9
Body
Row 8
Row 7
Row 6
Row 5
Row 4
Row 3
Row 2
Row 1

} 22 pcs. in each row

Center front
Join ends to form a ring of 22 pcs.

Bow

1"
Marking pin
2¾"
Bead wheel

How to make Bill

Bill
Slit to the middle.
→

Signs for piece direction

△	Double pocket	▽	Double pocket	∧	Double pocket	∨	Double pocket	▽	Insert here.

❶

Apply a dab of glue on single points of 5-6 pcs., and paste them together. Repeat to make this set until 22 pcs. are used.

❷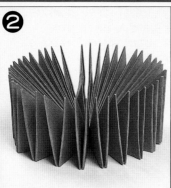

Paste each other and join into a circle of 22 pcs. (Row 1).

❸

Row 2: Insert adjoining points of Row 1 into double pocket of a piece, double points facing up. Continue all around.

❹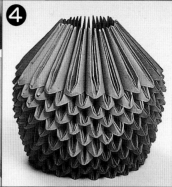

Rows 3-12: Continue joining the same number of pieces, altering color as directed on the opposite page.

❺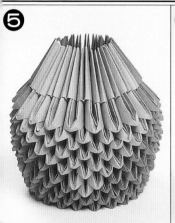

Row 13: Shape neck by changing direction of pieces, the right angles facing outward. See diagram for colors.

❻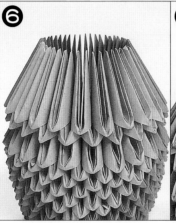

Rows 14-16: Change direction of pieces again, and work as directed on the color chart.

❼

Insert bill (red) into Row 16.

❽

Row 17: Work in the same manner as the previous row.

❾

Row 18: Form ears; change direction of pieces and work only on ears.

❿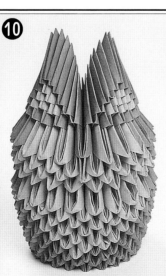

Both ears are completed.

⓫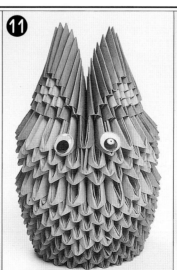

Glue on eyes.

⓬

Attach bow and bead wheel by pushing in marking pin.

#77–#79 FLOWER GIRL & RING BEARER (P.26)

Completed size
2¾" wide, 3" high

Materials

	⟨#77⟩	[#78]	|#79|
274 1⅛"×2⅛" rectangles of craft paper	⟨yellow⟩	[blue]	|pink|
88 1⅛"×2⅛" rectangles of craft paper	⟨white⟩	[white]	|white|
1 1⅛"×2⅛" rectangle of craft paper	⟨red⟩	[red]	|red|
1 pearl-headed marking pin	⟨yellow⟩	[blue]	|pink|
3" ⅓" ribbon	⟨silver⟩	[silver]	|silver|
1 ½" diam. bead wheel	⟨gold⟩	[gold]	|gold|
5 stemmed silk flowers plus 1 stemmed bud each			

2 ½" diam. plastic eyes each
5"×8" tulle (for #79)
2 silk flowers (for #79)

Ear

Silk flower attaching position for #79

Eye attaching position

Bill(red)

Bow attaching position

Bouquet attaching position

Body

△ ·········· Row 22 (2 pcs.)
△△ △△ ·········· Row 21 (4 pcs.)
△▲▲△ △▲△ ·········· Row 20 (6 pcs.)
△▲▲△ △▲▲△ ·········· Row 19 (8 pcs.)
△▲▲▲△ △▲▲▲△ ·········· Row 18 (10 pcs.)
△△△△△△ △△△△△△ ·········· Row 17 (12 pcs.)
▽▽▽▽▽▽▼▼▼▼▽▼▼▼▽▽▽▽▽▽ ···· Row 16
▽▽▽▽▽▼▼▼▼▼▼▼▽▽▽▽▽▽ ···· Row 15
▽▽▽▽▽▼▼▼▼▼▼▼▽▽▽▽▽▽ ···· Row 14
▽▽▽▽▽▼▼▼▼▼▼▼▽▽▽▽▽▽ ···· Row 13
△△△△△▲▲▲▲▲▲▲△△△△△△△ ←·· Row 12   Neck
▽▽▽▽▽▼▼▼▼▼▼▽▽▽▽▽▽▽ ···· Row 11
▽▽▽▽▽▼▼▼▼▼▼▽▽▽▽▽▽▽ ···· Row 10
▽▽▽▽▽▼▼▼▼▼▼▽▽▽▽▽▽▽ ···· Row 9
▽▽▽▽▽▽▼▼▼▼▽▽▽▽▽▽▽ ···· Row 8
▽▽▽▽▽▽▼▼▼▼▽▽▽▽▽▽▽ ···· Row 7
▽▽▽▽▽▽▽▼▼▼▽▽▽▽▽▽▽ ···· Row 6
▽▽▽▽▽▽▽▼▼▽▽▽▽▽▽▽ ···· Row 5
▽▽▽▽▽▽▽▽▼▽▽▽▽▽▽▽ ···· Row 4
▽▽▽▽▽▽▽▽▽▽▽▽▽▽▽▽ ···· Row 3
▽▽▽▽▽▽▽▽▽▽▽▽▽▽▽▽ ···· Row 2
△△△△△△△△△△△△△△△△△△△△△ ···· Row 1

} 20 pcs. in each row

↑ Center front
Join ends to form a ring of 20 pcs.

△ Yellow for #77
Blue for #78
Pink for #79

▲ White

Bow

1"

Bead wheel
Marking pin

Bouquet

Stemmed silk flower

1¼"

Bud

Bind with floral tape.

½"

⬅See P.77 for step-by-step instructions.

How to make Bill

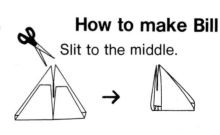

Slit to the middle.

→

● For veil, see P.75
Signs for piece direction

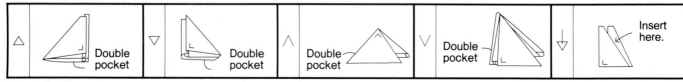

| △ | Double pocket | ▽ | Double pocket | ∧ | Double pocket | ∨ | Double pocket | ⬇ | Insert here. |

78

#1 GRANNY OWL (P.3)

Completed size
2¼" wide, 4" high

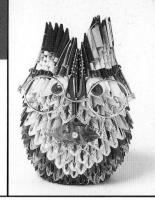

Materials
- 328 1½" × 2¼" rectangles of glossy paper (black shades)
- 88 1½" × 2¼" rectangles of glossy paper (white base)
- 1 1½" × 2¼" rectangle of glossy paper (red shades)
- 2 ½" diam. plastic eyes
- 1 pearl-headed marking pin (white)
- 2" #28 wrapped wire (green)
- 1 pair doll's glasses

△ Magazine paper in black shades

▲ Magazine paper with white base

Ear

△ ·········· Row 23 (2 pcs.)
△△　△△ ·········· Row 22 (4 pcs.)
△▲△　△▲△ ·········· Row 21 (6 pcs.)
△▲▲△　△▲▲△ ·········· Row 20 (8 pcs.)

Glass attaching position
△▲▲▲△　△▲▲▲△ ·········· Row 19 (10 pcs.)
△△△△△△△△△△△△ ·········· Row 18 (12 pcs.)

Eye attaching position
▽▽▽▽▽▽▽▽▼▼▼▼▼▼▽▽▽▽▽▽▽▽ ·········· Row 17

▽▽▽▽▽▽▼▼▼▼▼▼▽▽▽▽▽▽ ·········· Row 16

▽▽▽▽▽▼▼▼▼▼▼▼▽▽▽▽▽ ·········· Row 15

▽▽▽▽▼▼▼▼▼▼▼▼▽▽▽▽ ·········· Row 14

Neck △△△△△△△▲▲▲▲▲▲▲▲▲△△△△△△△ ← ·········· Row 13

Body
▽▽▽▽▽▼▼▼▼▼▼▽▽▽▽▽ ·········· Row 12

▽▽▽▽▽▽▼▼▼▼▼▽▽▽▽▽▽ ·········· Row 11

Leaf attaching position
▽▽▽▽▽▽▽▼▼▼▼▼▽▽▽▽▽▽▽ ·········· Row 10

▽▽▽▽▽▽▽▽▼▼▼▼▽▽▽▽▽▽▽▽ ·········· Row 9

▽▽▽▽▽▽▽▽▽▼▼▼▽▽▽▽▽▽▽▽▽ ·········· Row 8

▽▽▽▽▽▽▽▽▽▽▼▼▼▽▽▽▽▽▽▽▽▽ ·········· Row 7

▽▽▽▽▽▽▽▽▽▽▼▼▽▽▽▽▽▽▽▽▽▽ ·········· Row 6

▽▽▽▽▽▽▽▽▽▽▼▽▽▽▽▽▽▽▽▽▽▽ ·········· Row 5

▽▽▽▽▽▽▽▽▽▽▽▽▽▽▽▽▽▽▽▽▽▽ ·········· Row 4

▽▽▽▽▽▽▽▽▽▽▽▽▽▽▽▽▽▽▽▽▽▽ ·········· Row 3

▽▽▽▽▽▽▽▽▽▽▽▽▽▽▽▽▽▽▽▽▽▽ ·········· Row 2

△△△△△△△△△△△△△△△△△△△△△△ → Row 1

22 pcs. in each row

Center front

Join ends to form a ring of 22 pcs.

Leaf (Actual size)
Attach with marking pin.

Bill(red)

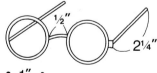

Reading glasses

Doll's glasses are used here, but if not available, make a pair with a piece of wire.

½"　2¼"
← 1" →

How to attach hook for glasses

Hook

Piece

Insert with glue.

⅛"

Join pieces in the same manner as for #62-64 OWL on P.77.

How to make Bill

Slit to the middle.

½

→

← See P.77 for step-by-step instructions.

79

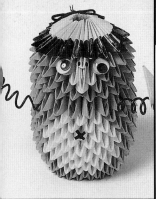

#68 KAPPA (P.25)

Materials
250 2⅜" × 4¼" rectangles of craft paper (pale green)
 75 2⅜" × 4¼" rectangles of craft paper (black)
 58 2⅜" × 4¼" rectangles of craft paper (yellow) + 2 pcs. for hands
 20 1⅛" × 4¼" rectangles of craft paper (yellow, for rain hat)
  1 1½" × 4" rectangle of craft paper (black, for hair ornament)
 55 4¼" × 1⅛" rectangles of tissue paper (black)
8" ¹⁄₁₆" cord (purple)
Felt (black) for nostrils and navel
1 ft. ¹⁄₁₆" wire (bronze)

∗ 55 of 75 black pcs. are used to construct back of body. When folding these pieces, layer black tissue paper to give thickness.
∗ When folding pieces for rain hat as instructed on P.29, cut rectangles lengthwise in half, omit the first folding, and start from Step 2.

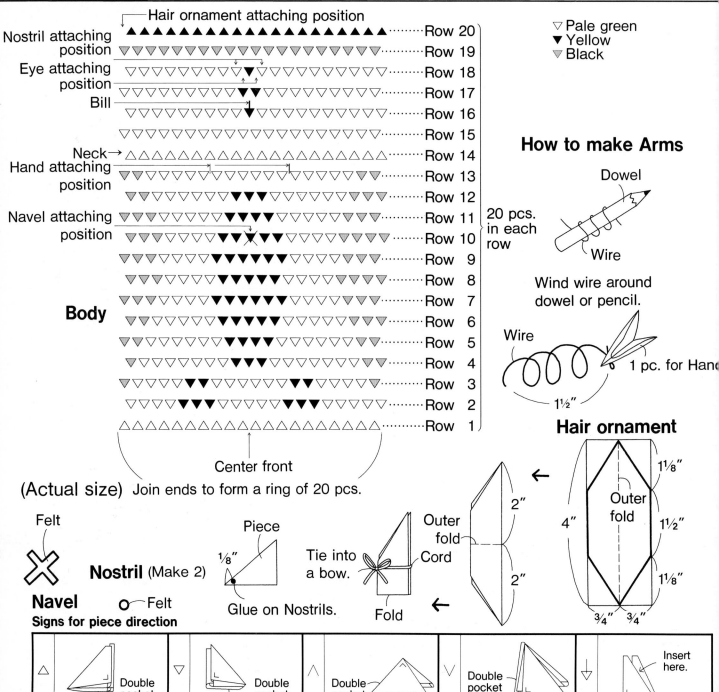

Hair ornament attaching position

Nostril attaching position .... Row 20
 .... Row 19
Eye attaching position .... Row 18
 .... Row 17
Bill .... Row 16
 .... Row 15
Neck→ .... Row 14
Hand attaching position .... Row 13
 .... Row 12
Navel attaching position .... Row 11
 .... Row 10
 .... Row 9
 .... Row 8
Body .... Row 7
 .... Row 6
 .... Row 5
 .... Row 4
 .... Row 3
 .... Row 2
 .... Row 1

▽ Pale green
▼ Yellow
▽ Black

20 pcs. in each row

Center front

(Actual size) Join ends to form a ring of 20 pcs.

How to make Arms

Dowel
Wire

Wind wire around dowel or pencil.

Wire
1 pc. for Hand
1½"

Hair ornament

1⅛"
Outer fold
2"
4"
1½"
2"
1⅛"
¾" ¾"

Outer fold
Cord

Tie into a bow.
Fold

Felt
✗
Nostril (Make 2)
⅛"
Piece
Glue on Nostrils.

Navel ○—Felt
Signs for piece direction

△ Double pocket	▽ Double pocket	∧ Double pocket	∨ Double pocket	↓ Insert here.

❶

Apply a dab of glue on single points of 5-6 pcs., and paste them together. Repeat to make this set until 20 pcs. are used.

❷

Paste each other and join into a circle of 20 pcs. (Row 1).

❸

Row 2: Insert adjoining points of Row 1 into double pocket of a piece, double points facing up. Continue all around.

❹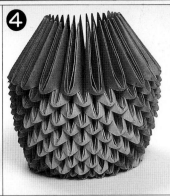

Rows 3-13: Continue joining the same number of pieces, altering color as directed on the opposite page.

❺

Row 14: Shape neck by changing direction of pieces, the right angles facing outward.

❻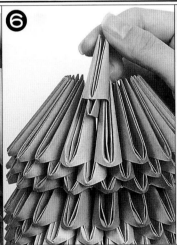

Rows 15-17: Change direction of pieces again, and work as directed. Insert bill (yellow) into Row 17.

❼

Row 18: Work in the same manner as the previous row, altering colors as directed.

❽

Row 19: Make hair by joining 20 black pcs.

❾

Row 20: Make rain hat by joining 20 yellow pcs.

Insert hair ornament into center back of Row 20.

⓫

Glue on eyes and felt nostrils. Glue felt navel onto Row 10.

⓬

Make arms and hands with wire and triangles, and insert into body.

#69 & #70 PENGUIN (P.25)

Materials ⟨#69⟩ [#70]

304 2⅜" × 4¼" rectangles of craft paper ⟨black⟩ [blue]
48 2⅜" × 4¼" rectangles of craft paper ⟨blue⟩ [white]
7 2⅜" × 4¼" rectangles of craft paper ⟨yellow⟩ [yellow]
3 2⅜" × 4¼" rectangles of craft paper ⟨black⟩ [blue]
           for wing and feet
1 1¼" × 2¾" rectangle of craft paper ⟨yellow⟩ [yellow] for bill

(Following materials are for each item.
4" ⅓" ribbon (red)
2 ½" diam. plastic eyes
1 straw hat for dolls

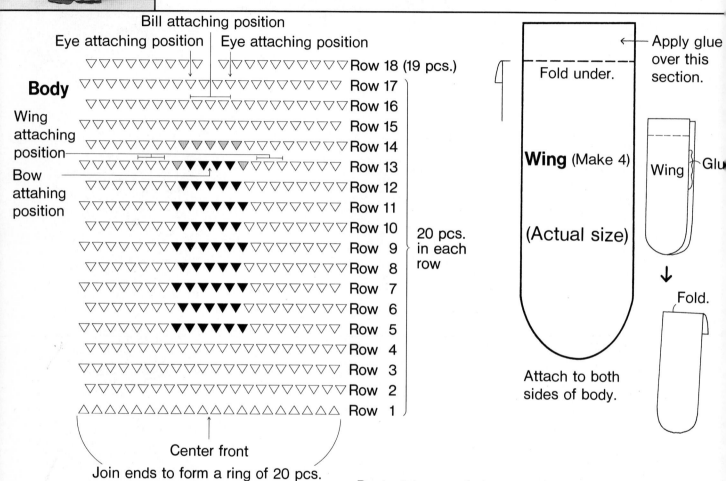

Body

Bill attaching position
Eye attaching position | Eye attaching position

Row 18 (19 pcs.)
Row 17
Row 16
Row 15
Row 14
Row 13
Row 12
Row 11
Row 10
Row 9
Row 8
Row 7
Row 6
Row 5
Row 4
Row 3
Row 2
Row 1

Wing attaching position

Bow attaching position

20 pcs. in each row

Center front
Join ends to form a ring of 20 pcs.

Fold under.

Apply glue over this section.

Wing (Make 4)

(Actual size)

Wing | Glu(e)

Fold.

Attach to both sides of body.

▽ Black for **#69**/Blue for **#70**
▼ Blue for **#69**/White for **#70**
▽ Yellow

Bow tie

1⅛"

Paste 2 layers of sheets and cut out.

Feet (Actual size)

Section for gluing | Feet

Outline of Body

Paste 2 layers together.

Signs for piece direction

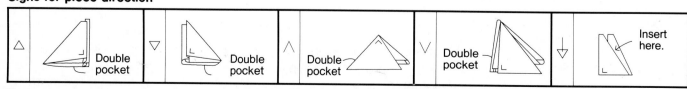

| △ | Double pocket | ▽ | Double pocket | ∧ | Double pocket | ∨ | Double pocket | ↓ | Insert here. |

❶

Apply a dab of glue on single points of 5-6 pcs., and paste them together. Repeat to make this set until 20 pcs. are used.

❷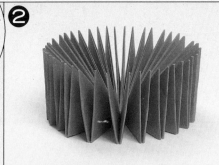

Paste each other and join into a circle of 20 pcs. (Row 1).

❸

Row 2: Insert adjoining points of Row 1 into double pocket of a piece, double points facing up. Continue all around.

❹

Rows 3-18: Join 20 each pcs. in the same manner, altering colors as directed in the diagram.

❺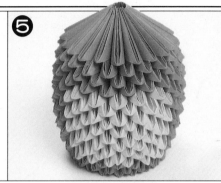

Check the shape. Interlock so the top opening is as small as possible.

❻

Glue on eyes and bow tie.

❼

Make bill as directed below, and glue onto the indicated position.

❽

Make wings and feet. Glue onto body.

❾

Glue on straw hat to finish.

How to make Bill

Fold a 1¼" × 2¾" rectangular paper in half.

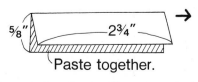

5/8"   2¾"

Paste together.

Inner fold

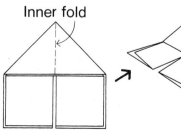

Fold down corners to meet at the center bottom, and secure upper half with glue.

Base

Fold down in half and unfold.

Base

Overlap squares and glue together.

#71 & #72 KITTEN (P.25)

Completed size
4″ wide, 5½″ high

Materials

	‹#71›	[#72]
220 2⅜″ × 4¼″ rectangles of craft paper	‹yellow›	[green]
134 2″ × 3½″ rectangles of craft paper	‹yellow›	[green]
1 ¾″ × ¾″ rectangle of craft paper	‹black›	[black] for ear
6″ wired tinsel	‹yellow›	[brown]

(Following materials are for each item)
20″ ⅓″ ribbon (pink)
2 ½″ diam. plastic eyes
1 miniature bell
1½ ft. #28 wrapped wire
   (white, for whiskers)
1 ⅓″ diam. button (black)

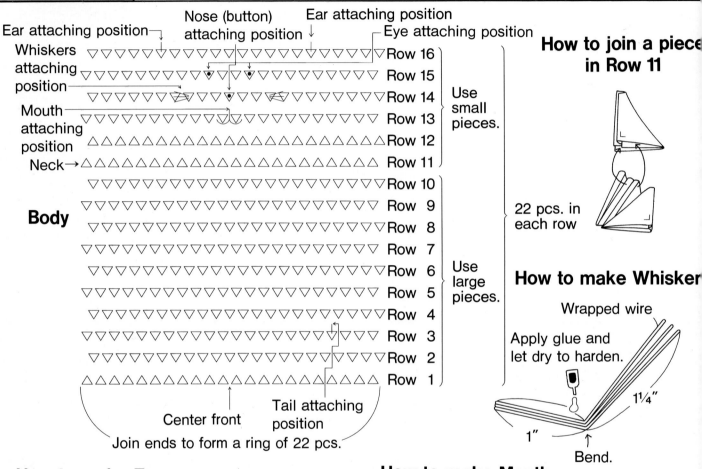

Ear attaching position
Nose (button) attaching position
Ear attaching position
Eye attaching position

Whiskers attaching position

Mouth attaching position

Neck →

Row 16
Row 15
Row 14
Row 13
Row 12
Row 11

Use small pieces.

Body

Row 10
Row 9
Row 8
Row 7
Row 6
Row 5
Row 4
Row 3
Row 2
Row 1

Use large pieces.

Center front
Tail attaching position
Join ends to form a ring of 22 pcs.

How to join a piece in Row 11

22 pcs. in each row

How to make Whisker

Wrapped wire
Apply glue and let dry to harden.
1¼″
1″
Bend.

How to make Ear

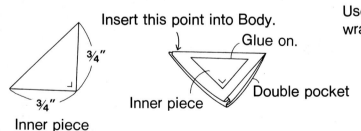

Insert this point into Body.
Glue on.
¾″
¾″
Inner piece
Double pocket
Inner piece

How to make Mouth

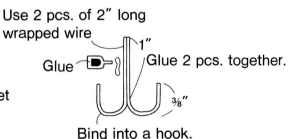

Use 2 pcs. of 2″ long wrapped wire
Glue
1″
Glue 2 pcs. together.
⅜″
Bind into a hook.

❶ Apply a dab of glue on single points of 5-6 large pcs., and paste them together. Repeat to make this set until 22 pcs. are used.

❷ Paste each other and join into a circle of 22 pcs. (Row 1).

❸ Row 2: Insert adjoining points of Row 1 into double pocket of a piece, double points facing up. Continue all around.

❹ Rows 3-10: Join 22 each pcs. in the same manner.

❺ Row 11: Using small pieces, shape neck by changing direction of pieces, so the right angles face outward.

❻ Row 12: Work as for Row 11 with small pieces. Row 13: Change direction of pieces again.

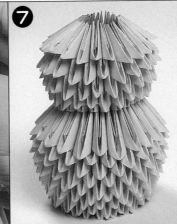

❼ Rows 13-17: Work in the same manner with small pieces, shaping into a ball.

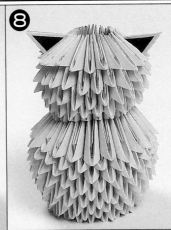

❽ Make ears as directed and insert between 4th and 5th pcs. from center front of Row 17.

❾ Make mouth with wire as directed, and insert into center front of Row 14.

❿ Make 2 whiskers using wire, and insert into both sides of nose.

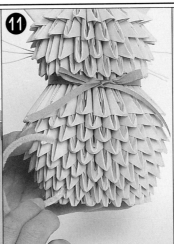

⓫ Attach bell onto center of ribbon, and tie around neck into a bow. Insert wired tinsel as tail.

⓬ Glue eyes and nose onto indicated positions.

#73 & #74 RABBIT (P.25)

Materials

	‹#73›	[#74]
292 2"×3½" rectangles of craft paper	‹white›	[pale pink]
14 2"×3½" rectangles of thin craft paper	‹pink›	[pink]
1 2"×3½" rectangle of craft paper	‹red›	[red]

1 pearl-headred marking pin
(Following materials are for each item.)
1 ½" diam. button (black)
2 ½" diam. buttons (red)
8" ¼" ribbon (red)

1½ ft. #28 wrapped wire
(white, for whiskers)
1 ½" bead wheel (gold)

*When folding thin craft paper
as instructed on P.29, cut rectangles lengthwise in half, omit
the first folding, and start from
Step 2.

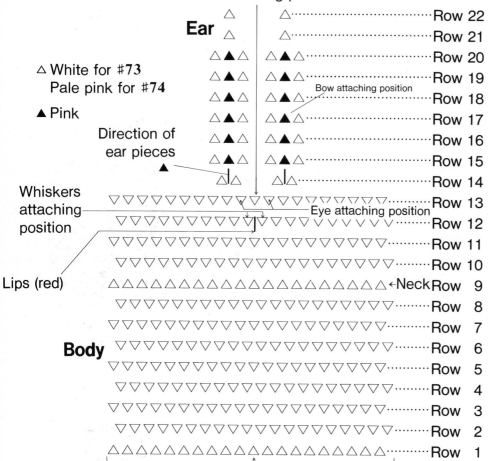

Nose attaching position

Ear

△ White for #73
Pale pink for #74

▲ Pink

Direction of ear pieces

Whiskers attaching position

Lips (red)

Body

Row 22
Row 21
Row 20
Row 19
Row 18
Row 17
Row 16
Row 15
Row 14

Bow attaching position

Row 13
Row 12
Row 11
Row 10
Row 9 ←Neck
Row 8
Row 7
Row 6
Row 5
Row 4
Row 3
Row 2
Row 1

Eye attaching position

Center front
Join ends to form a ring of 20 pcs.

How to make Whiskers

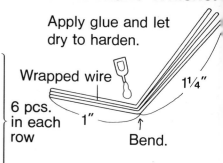

Apply glue and let dry to harden.

Wrapped wire

6 pcs. in each row

1¼"

1"

Bend.

Ear

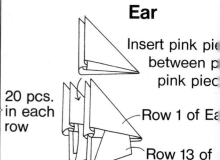

Insert pink pie
between p
pink piec

20 pcs. in each row

Row 1 of Ea

Row 13 of

↓

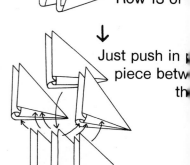

Just push in
piece betw
th

Divide 3 pcs. into 2 (3 points each
and insert into 2 pcs.

Bow

Marking pin

¾"
Bead wheel

1"

Signs for piece direction

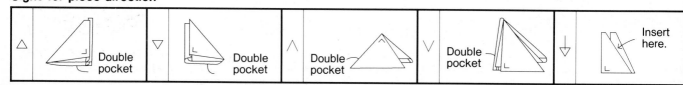

| △ Double pocket | ▽ Double pocket | ∧ Double pocket | ∨ Double pocket | ↓ Insert here. |

① Apply a dab of glue on single points of 5-6 pcs., and paste them together. Repeat to make this set until 20 pcs. are used.

② Paste all sets together and join into a circle of 20 pcs. (Row 1).

③ Row 2: Insert adjoining points of Row 1 into double pocket of a piece, double points facing up. Continue all around.

④ Rows 3-8: Join 20 each pieces in the same manner.

⑤ Row 9: Shape neck by changing direction of pieces.

⑥ Rows 10-12: Change direction of pieces again, and continue in the same manner.

⑦ Push in a beak piece (red) between center 2 pcs. of Row 12.

⑧ Row 13: Work in the same manner, using 20 pcs.

⑨ Shape ears by changing direction of pieces. Join 2 each pcs., sandwiching 1 pink piece.

⑩ Rows 21-22: Join 1 pc. each, covering only the center 2 points.

⑪ Glue on eyes and nose. Make whiskers referring to the figure on the opposite page, and insert into the sides of lips.

⑫ Attach bow and bead wheel using a marking pin.

#55 & #56 METALLIC URN (P.22)

Completed size
5½" wide, 8½" hig.

Materials
#55: 916 1½"×2¾" rectangles of craft paper (gold)
    2 ft. ¾" ribbon (gold)
#56: 916 1½"×2¾" rectangles of craft paper (silver)
    2 ft. ¾" ribbon (silver)

Note
The completed project may look different depending on the thickness of the paper used.

URN

△△△△△△△△△△△△△△△△△△△△△△△△△△△△△△△△△△ ·············Row 21 (32
△△△△△△△△△△△△△△△△△△△△△△△△△△△△△△△△△△△ ············Row 20 (32
△△△△△△△△△△△△△△△△△△△△△△△△△△△△△△△△△△△△ ···········Row 19 (32
△△△△△△△△△△△△△△△△△△△△△△△△△△△△△△△△△△△△△△△Row 18

Handle attaching position

△△△△△△△△△△△△△△△△△△△△△△△△△△△△△△△△△△△△△△△··Row 17
△△Row 16
△△△△△△△△△△△△△△△△△△△△△△△△△△△△△△△△△△△△△△△··Row 15
△△Row 14
△△△△△△△△△△△△△△△△△△△△△△△△△△△△△△△△△△△△△△△··Row 13
△△Row 12
△△△△△△△△△△△△△△△△△△△△△△△△△△△△△△△△△△△△△△△··Row 11
△△Row 10
△△△△△△△△△△△△△△△△△△△△△△△△△△△△△△△△△△△△△△△··Row 9
△△△△△△△△△△△△△△△△△△△△△△△△△△△△△△△△△△△△△△△··Row 8
△△△△△△△△△△△△△△△△△△△△△△△△△△△△△△△△△△△△△△△··Row 7
△△Row 6
△△··Row 5
▽▽▽▽▽▽▽▽▽▽▽▽▽▽▽▽▽▽▽▽▽▽▽▽▽▽▽▽▽▽▽▽▽▽▽▽▽···Row 4
▽▽▽▽▽▽▽▽▽▽▽▽▽▽▽▽▽▽▽▽▽▽▽▽▽▽▽▽▽▽▽▽▽▽▽▽··Row 3

Change direction of pieces here.

△△Row 2
▽▽▽▽▽▽▽▽▽▽▽▽▽▽▽▽▽▽▽▽▽▽▽▽▽▽▽▽▽▽▽▽▽▽▽▽▽▽Row 1

└─ Center

Join ends to form a ring of 40 pcs. (¾" inner diameter.)

Pedestal

▷ ▷
▷ ▷

├───Join 30 pcs. into a ring of 2" in diameter. Make 2 and glue together.───┤

Pedestal assembly

Place URN on the pedestal and secure with glue.

➡See P.90 for step-by-step instructions.

Signs for piece direction

△	Double pocket	▽	Double pocket	∧	Double pocket	∨	Double pocket	↓	Insert here.

Rows 1-2 assembly

Direction of pieces

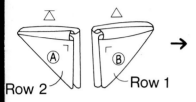

Row 2

Row 1

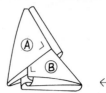

This side becomes the bottom.

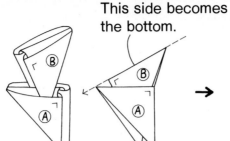

B

B

A

A

→

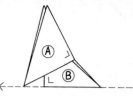

A

A

B

B

Turn upside down.
This pair makes 1 pc. for Row 1.
Make 40 pairs and join into a ring.

How to decrease number of pieces

Repeat this pattern.

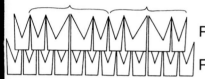

Row 19
Row 18

Row 3 assembly

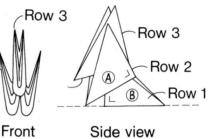

Row 3

Row 3

Row 3

Row 2

Row 2

A

B

Row 1

Front

Side view

Row 5 assembly

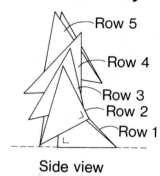

Row 5

Row 4

Row 3

Row 2

Row 1

Side view

Handle (20 pcs.)

How to attach Handle

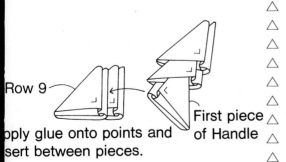

Row 18

End of Handle

Apply glue onto points and insert between pieces.

Row 9

First piece of Handle

Apply glue onto points and insert between pieces.

△
△
△
△
△
△
△
△
△
△
△
△
△
△
△
△
△
△
△
▽

Handle assembly

First piece of Handle

Handle
(Actual size)

(Make 2)

Shape according to the pattern (right)

First piece of Handle

89

❶

Make a 2-pc. set interlocked as directed overleaf. Repeat and prepare 40 sets.

❷

Put a set upside down. This makes Row 1 and Row 2.

❸

Showing the interlocking direction of a Row 3 piece.

❹

Join a pair of set by inserting adjoining points into a new piece.

❺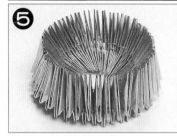

Continue to join all 40 sets, into a ring.

❻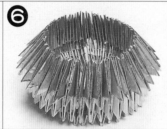

Row 4: Work in the same manner, with 40 pcs.

❼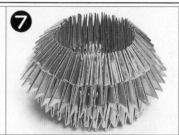

Row 5: Change the direction of pieces, the right angles facing out.

❽

Rows 5-6: Join pieces at an angle so the opening is 1¾"-2" in diam., securing with glue.

❾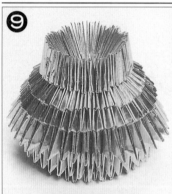

Row 7: Pieces are joined almost vertically.

❿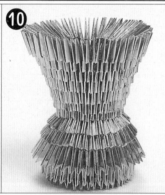

Rows 8-13: Work in the same manner, this time expanding the diam. gradually.

⓫

Rows 14-18: Work in the same manner, reducing the diam.

⓬

Rows 19-20: Decrease the number of pieces to 32, referring to the figure overleaf.

⓭

Row 21: Work in the same manner, slightly enlarging the opening to form rim.

⓮

Make pedestal and handles as directed.

⓯

Attach handles to sides. Glue pedestal and the bottom of the URN together.

⓰

Tie a ribbon around the neck to finish.